SYNODICAL GOVERNMENT IN THE CHURCH OF ENGLAND:
A Review

The report of the review group
appointed by the Standing Committee
of the General Synod

CHURCH HOUSE
PUBLISHING

Church House Publishing,
Church House,
Great Smith Street,
London SW1P 3NZ

ISBN 0 7151 3806 5

Published 1997 for the General Synod of the Church of England by
Church House Publishing

Cover design by Leigh Hurlock

Printed in England by The Cromwell Press Ltd, Melksham, Wiltshire

Contents

Members of the Group

Lord Bridge of Harwich (Chairman)
A former Lord of Appeal in Ordinary and Chairman of the Ecclesiastical Committee of Parliament from 1982 to 1992

The Rt Revd Alan Chesters (Vice-Chairman)
Bishop of Blackburn

The Revd Canon Bob Baker
Rector of Brundall, Braydeston and Postwick, Norwich; Church Commissioner; member of General Synod; former Rural Dean and Chairman of House of Clergy, Norwich Diocesan Synod

Professor Michael Clarke (from November 1995)
Head of the School of Public Policy at the University of Birmingham; Member of General Synod 1990–3, 1995– ; former Churchwarden and Deanery Lay Chairman

Sir John Herbecq KCB
Church Commissioner 1982–96; Chairman of Chichester Diocesan Board of Finance; member of the Chichester Diocesan Synod; former Churchwarden

Mrs Sarah James (until November 1995)
Reader; member of the General Synod; Vice-Chairman of the Central Readers Council; former Deanery Lay Chairman

Baroness McFarlane of Llandaff
Emeritus Professor – Manchester University; former Churchwarden; former member of the General Synod, of Deanery and Diocesan Synods and of PCC

Mr Michael Mockridge
Former partner of the solicitors, Clifford Chance; Trustee of the Church Urban Fund

Assessors
Mr Philip Mawer
Secretary-General of the General Synod

Mr Brian Hanson CBE
Legal Adviser to the General Synod

Mr Peter Mills
Diocesan Secretary: Diocese of Chester

Secretary
Mr Nigel Barnett
General Synod Office

Assistant Secretary
Ms Shirley Davies (until October 1996)

Chairman's Preface

1   We were appointed in April 1993. As I write this preface, the hope is that our report will be published this summer. I regret that our work should have taken four years to complete. At our first meeting in May 1993 we agreed a provisional timetable aiming at the production of our report by the end of 1995 or early in 1996. During the summer of 1993 a great deal of evidence was gathered by the secretariat and analysed for us. But before we met for the second time to consider this, the Lambeth Group had reported in July 1993 and their report recommended that: 'It would be appropriate for the Church to review its overall organisational structure in the light of its present-day activities and requirements.' This recommendation led, as was foreseeable, to the fundamental review undertaken by the Archbishops' Commission on the Organisation of the Church of England (the Turnbull Commission) of which I had the honour to be a member.

2   It was clear from the outset that there would be a significant overlap between our work in the Review of Synodical Government and the work of the Turnbull Commission. A comparison of our terms of reference with theirs bears this out. Until the Turnbull Commission reached final conclusions in 1995, we did not feel able to reach even provisional conclusions except on relatively minor matters, although we employed this time, profitably I hope, in the essential ground work of gathering further evidence, particularly by making visits to dioceses which proved a most fruitful exercise. But the crucial business of reaching our conclusions about the recommendations we should make has all been undertaken in the last eighteen months. I am comforted to be reassured that, in so far as our recommendations are accepted, it should still be possible for the necessary legislation to be brought forward in the lifetime of the present General Synod.

3   If there has been an unacceptable delay in the production of our report, a compensating gain has been the assistance we have derived from considering the principles expressed in the Turnbull Report. It goes without saying that what we are all trying to do is to discern the will of God for his Church. I hope and believe that the two reports are consistent and mutually complementary.

4   I am very conscious that our report, perhaps more than most of its kind, will be found rather heavy going for many readers. This, I believe, is primarily because our exposition of the main changes we recommend, and of the rationale for them, is interspersed with a good deal of necessary but relatively minor detail of limited interest. The principal changes recommended are the removal of deanery synods from the statutory structure of synodical government, the abolition of the Convocations, the substantial reduction in the size of the General Synod, the abolition of most special constituencies in it and the replacement of lay members of deanery synods as electors of the houses of laity of diocesan synods and the General Synod by a new body of synodical electors themselves elected by the parishes to perform that sole function. We summarise our conclusions and recommendations in Chapter 13.

5   My debt of gratitude to the other members of the Group is incalculable. They have all contributed most generously of their time and energy to our deliberations. I express my special thanks to the Bishop of Blackburn as Vice-Chairman.

6   Next, my warmest thanks are due to our assessors. Philip Mawer's unrivalled understanding of the way in which Church government works and of its strengths and weaknesses, coupled with his outstanding ability to help us to articulate our ideas accurately, have been invaluable. Peter Mills is a mine of information about everything that happens at diocesan level of which we have had the benefit and without which we should have been constantly in danger of falling into error. Brian Hanson has been always ready with a solution to our legal conundrums.

7   Last but not least my cordial thanks go to our secretary, Nigel Barnett, and to Shirley Davies who was his able assistant until she moved from Church House to the diocese of York in October last year. Nigel has worked tirelessly to produce successive drafts of our report and is entitled to a large share of any credit which is due for the editorship and style of the final version.

Bridge of Harwich

Lord Bridge of Harwich
Maundy Thursday 1997

1

Introduction

1.1   Views within the Church of England about synodical government cover a wide spectrum. For some, it is one of the touchstones of a Church which gives all its members a say in the management of its affairs. For others, it is a recipe for disaster, licensing the proliferation of ecclesiastical talking shops and encouraging religious busybodies.

1.2   Government by synods or councils goes back to the earliest days of the universal Church. In the Anglican Communion, however, it has, for more than 100 years, taken a particular form, in which representatives of clergy and laity have joined with bishops in overseeing the affairs of the Church. The continuing experiment in vesting significant authority in a body or bodies consisting of bishops and representative clergy and laity is of great significance not only to the Church of England but to all other Churches.

1.3   For synodical government is not only or even primarily about finding a set of convenient organisational arrangements for the administration of the Church; it is also about theological principles. At its heart is the notion that all Christians are equally members of the Body of Christ, and entitled to be represented in its government. As the report of the Lowe Commission put it in 1958[1] (see also Appendix I, paragraph 17):

> '. . . theology justifies, and history demonstrates, . . . that the ultimate authority and right of collective action lie with the whole body, the Church; and that the co-operation of clergy and laity in Church government and discipline belongs to the true ideal of the Church.'

1.4   We elaborate in Chapters 2 and 3 on this and other principles on which synodical government is based. In doing so, we identify two other principles of key importance to any understanding of synodical government in the Church of England:

---

1   *The Convocations and the Laity*, C.A. 1240, Church Information Board, 1958.

1

- the role of bishops as guardians of the worship and doctrine of the Church. This is reflected in synodical government by the requirement that matters relating to the formulation of doctrine and to the sacraments and services of the Church should be submitted for final approval by the General Synod in terms proposed by the House of Bishops; and

- under the law of Church and State, each province and every diocese has pastoral authority within its own territorial area.

Although their practical application has occasionally been criticised, our researches suggest that these principles are still appropriate.

1.5   Although these principles are of long standing, synodical government as such in the Church of England is a relatively recent innovation. It came into existence with the passage of the Synodical Government Measure 1969 (the 1969 Measure) and the inauguration of the General Synod the following year. Its roots go back much further, however, as we describe in Appendix I of our report.

1.6   The particular form which synodical government takes in the Church of England reflects both theological principle and the particular history of that Church. In 1985 the General Synod agreed that, some 20 years after the passing of the 1969 Measure, it would be appropriate to look at synodical government in all its forms – from the parochial church council (PCC) through to the General Synod – to see how well those forms operate.

1.7   The context in which synodical government functions has changed significantly even since the discussion paper which inaugurated the present review was issued in 1990.[2] In Chapter 3 we identify some of those changes and their implications. They include:

- a growing awareness of the primacy of mission in the life of the contemporary church;

- the increasing emphasis on the parish as the base from which the resources of the Church are gathered;

---

2   *Synodical Government 1970–1990; The First Twenty Years* – GS Misc 344, Church House Publishing, 1990.

- the growing need for systems of government which carry the confidence of dioceses and parishes, and which model subsidiarity and accountability in the way they work;

- a corresponding need for those systems to hold before parishes the interests and concerns of the wider Church of which they are part.

1.8 Recent years have also seen an understandable desire to improve the administration of the Church at national level. Recommendations to this effect were embodied in the report of the Archbishops' Commission on the Organisation of the Church of England (the Turnbull Report). While forming our own view on the issues before us, we have sought to ensure that our recommendations are compatible with the follow-up to that report, and to build on and complement the changes already under way wherever possible.

1.9 In the course of our work we have received much written evidence from dioceses, deaneries, parishes and others. We have also taken oral evidence in some instances, as well as visiting a number of dioceses to meet people involved in the synodical life of the Church at all levels, and others not formally part of this life. Details of the sources of our evidence are in Appendix II to our report. To all who have contributed to our review in any way, we offer our warm thanks.

1.10 Our findings and detailed recommendations are in Chapters 4–12. We begin by examining the operation of synodical government in the parish followed by the deanery, diocese and at the provincial and national level, ending with a look at the relationship between the General Synod and Parliament, and at communications between the different levels of synodical government. Our conclusions and recommendations are summarised in Chapter 13.

1.11 Overall, the evidence submitted to us suggests that there is wide acceptance of the general principles of synodical government and attachment to the general form it takes. Nevertheless, while the principles on which synodical government is founded are, we believe, still secure, the form in which they are expressed needs re-examination and adjustment. We have sought to base our recommendations for change on sound theology and factual evidence, and to ensure that

they are consistent with the Anglican tradition. Synodical government must, we believe, be reformed if the Church of England is
effectively to meet the opportunities and challenges it faces as it
enters the third millennium.

2

Theological principles
and historical development

The nature of the Church

2.1   The one, Holy, Catholic and Apostolic Church, of which the
Church of England is a part, has its origins in the creative, redeeming
and sanctifying work of the Holy Trinity. That understanding is fundamental to any consideration of the government of a body which the
Turnbull Report describes as an 'integral part of the mystery of God's
reconciling work in his world, and an embodiment of the presence of
God in the world. . . . The life of the Church in a rich and yet mysterious way is utterly trinitarian in its ground, being and hope.'
(paragraphs 1.1 and 1.6) All authority in the Church is ultimately
derived from the Triune God, Creator, Redeemer and Sanctifier of the
world.

2.2   The report of another Archbishops' Commission, the
Cameron Report[1] reminds us that 'to stress the Church is communal
is to emphasise relationships; the personal is thus prior to the structural, the institutional exists to nurture and sustain the relations of
human persons joined, as far as it is possible for us as creatures, in a
resemblance to that Trinitarian life.' (paragraph 19)

2.3   The New Testament contains a rich variety of images for the
Church. Among them the Church is described as the people of God,
as a holy nation, as a royal priesthood and as the Body of Christ.
Anglicans believe that all members of the Church have a responsibility
for the life and witness of the Church. It follows therefore that there
are appropriate ways in which all share in the process by which the
life of the Church is fashioned and its mission resourced.

---

1   *Episcopal Ministry* – GS 994, Church House Publishing, 1990.

Authority and the Church

2.4   Christ gave authority to his Church (John 20.21–23; Matthew 28.18–20). The ascended Lord has bestowed his gifts of leadership, teaching and pastoral care on the Church so that his people may be equipped for their particular ministry and to enable them to grow to full spiritual maturity (Ephesians 4. 7–16).

2.5   Christ entrusted authority for ministry to his people incorporated by their baptism into his mystical Body the Church. Every Christian shares in that ministerial authority by virtue of baptism. As such they are called to be prophets and to proclaim the wonderful deeds of their Saviour (1 Peter 2.9), to be priests and to offer the spiritual sacrifices of prayer, praise, gifts and finally themselves (1 Peter 2.5; Hebrews 13. 15–16), and as part of the royal priesthood to take their place in the government of Christ's Kingdom (1 Peter 2.9).

2.6   In the ordering of its life and in the exercise of authority the Church must seek to show and to uphold those characteristics of the divine authority revealed in Jesus Christ and recorded in Holy Scripture. In the Old Testament God is revealed as a sovereign Lord. Because he is sovereign he gives his people freedom. This self-limitation of God's power is the ground and guarantee of our human freedom and responsibility. In the New Testament the power of Christ is the power of the crucified Lord who has been raised from the dead. His power is employed in the service of that love which took him to the Cross. Any exercise of authority in the Church must conform to its source in Christ.

2.7   We share the theological understanding of the Turnbull Report that God in his goodness as his 'gracious gift' has given to the Church the resources it needs to be God's people and not least in that common fellowship we enjoy by baptism as members together of the Body of Christ (paragraphs 1.10 ff). We also share the conviction that the gifts given by the Holy Spirit 'are to be used in humility and love with attentiveness to the gifts and interests of others and with the goal of building up the whole Body and increasing its effectiveness.'

2.8   The community which acknowledges Christ as our Saviour possesses an innate longing for the communion with its Lord and with one another which is already given to it in Christ. However, in its life the Church is subject to the sinfulness and limitations of human nature. Because God has entrusted his authority into the hands of fallible human beings there is need for constant vigilance to ensure that that authority is always directed to the liberation and the building up of the people of God. It is an acknowledgement of the reality of sin which makes it necessary to have a set of checks and balances in the life of the Church, which will serve to prevent the abuse of power and to preserve the comprehensive nature of the Church.

2.9   In a divided Christendom it is impossible for any single Church to speak with the full authority of the Gospel. Churches can only legislate today for their own members knowing that there must necessarily be a provisional quality about their work. Nevertheless, decisions do have to be taken in the light of the best understanding possible and open always to the insights of other Christian communities.

2.10   Furthermore, because the Church of England is part of the Anglican Communion, whenever a matter touches the nature of that Communion particular attention has to be given to the understanding of other member Churches. We believe that our proposals are consistent with the ecclesiology of synodical government in other provinces of the Communion.

2.11   It has to be accepted that in the late twentieth century the authority of the Church, in practice, rests on its power to persuade its members and others to accept its teaching, moral guidance, and those regulations which order its life. Nevertheless, the Church does exercise authority over its clergy and those lay people who accept office in the Church, so that its mission and ministry are both enabled and sustained in its daily life. In practice, through the system of synodical government this is achieved by seeking to take that 'weighty counsel' in the General Synod which should be the hall mark of the Church and through that process of consultation at diocesan, deanery and parish level which reflects the expectations of members of the Church at grass roots level in a democratic society. In doing this the Church of England seeks to keep a balance between the international, national, regional and local aspects of Church life. The evidence we have considered suggests that synods carry conviction within the Church and in the wider society not only by the decisions they make but by the manner in which they make them.

2.12   Many see synodical government as a recovery in recent times of the original conviction that in the household of God decision-making requires full lay participation. Indeed, there is sufficient evidence in the records of the early Church for us to be confident that some representative laity were usually present at Councils. The process by which authority is exercised in the Church as in any other body can make or mar the reception of its final decisions. As W. Bright wrote in 1902: 'The *fideles* (faithful) have a clear right to say "We cannot accept this or that new doctrinal formula" – to veto it, in short.'[2] All decisions require eventually to be received by the whole Christian body and to achieve the status of a *consensus fidelium*, an agreement among the faithful.

'Episcopally led and synodically governed'

2.13   Within the Church some are ordained to particular liturgical, preaching and pastoral ministries and given authority to act to and for the whole Church. Among the Church's many and varied ministries is that of the exercise of *episcope* (oversight). Bishops exercise their role in relation to and in consultation with their priests, deacons and the lay people in their diocese (local church) as well as with their brother bishops. 'As a bishop I am set over you; as a Christian I am one of you' (Augustine of Hippo).[3] It is this understanding which has led to the Church of England being described as 'episcopally led and synodically governed' and to a serious attempt to express the inter-relation of the whole community in the government of the Church at parish, deanery, diocesan and national level. The Church has attempted this because it is convinced that such a system of government is based on the revelation of truth through scripture, tradition and reason.

2.14   The attempt to combine leadership by bishops with government of the Church by synods including representative clergy and

---

2   Letter of William Bright quoted in Eric Waldram Kemp, *Counsel and Consent. (Aspects of the Government of the Church as exemplified in the History of the English Provincial Synods)* (Bampton lectures for 1960), SPCK, 1961, page 215.

3   'Vobis enim sum episcopus, vobiscum sum Christianus'. St Augustine of Hippo, Sermon 340 from *Patrologiae cursus completus. Series latina,* edited by J.-P. Migne, volume 38 (1845), page 1483.

laity inevitably involves holding different forms of authority in tension. Bishops derive their authority from their orders and from tradition: it is not something bestowed on them by the institutional Church. To the authority inherent in their office is added the personal and public authority they acquire by their example and conduct. Moreover parishes and dioceses frequently demand leadership from their bishops. The last 20 years have, in the eyes of many, seen a very significant increase in the call for bishops to give leadership, whether in the synodical or in other aspects of the Church's life.

2.15   The authority of bishops cannot, however, be exercised in isolation from the rest of the Church. Leadership must be challenging and may be prophetic, but if it constantly fails to evoke a response it is ineffective. Synods provide a means through which the leadership given by bishops can be both tested and enabled. Synods too have their own sources of authority, derived not only or even primarily from their legal status but from their theological foundation, their representative character and their control of resources.

2.16   The phrase 'episcopally led and synodically governed' is one of those superficially attractive but ultimately misleading pieces of shorthand. It is misleading because it overlooks both the particular role of individual bishops and the House of Bishops in the Church's government (especially in relation to matters of doctrine and worship), and the potential leadership role of representative clergy and laity. It suggests that episcopal leadership is exercised outside the context of synodical government whereas it is often (though by no means solely) exercised within it. It ignores the subtlety and complexity of the relationship between bishop, clergy and laity.

2.17   At the end of the day the authority of the bishop and the authority of synods have to be held in a creative dialogue, which may perhaps be summed up by the model of the bishop-in-synod or bishop-in-council: the bishop leading in consultation and discussion with representative clergy and laity. As the Ordinal puts it:

> 'A bishop is called to lead in serving and caring for the people of God and to work with them in the oversight of the Church. As a chief pastor he shares with his fellow bishops a special responsibility to maintain and further the unity of the Church, to uphold its discipline, and to

guard its faith. He is to promote its mission throughout the world. It is his duty to watch over and pray for all those committed to his charge and to teach and govern them after the example of the Apostles, speaking in the name of God and interpreting the gospel of Christ. He is to know his people and be known by them. He is to ordain and to send new ministers, guiding those who serve with him and enabling them to fulfil their ministry.' (ASB, Ordinal, page 388)

The role of synods in the Church of England

2.18   The term synod is in origin a compound of two Greek words, *sun* meaning 'together' and *hodos* meaning 'the way', and was commonly used in Greek communities to describe their own system of assembling qualified citizens in order to discover the common will. Church synods were originally representative gatherings on a more local scale than a plenary Council and were usually regarded as able to make decisions only for those provinces or dioceses whose bishops and other representatives were present.

2.19   The Church of England believes it important to include all its members in the discernment of Christian truth and in the government of the Church. Synodical government is an attempt to seek and find the mind of Christ for his Church, as well as consensus in the ordering of the Church's life.

2.20   The particular form which synodical government takes in the Church of England reflects the history of the Church as well as theological principle. It has been affected in particular by the Church's relationship since the Reformation with Crown and Parliament. We sketch out the changing nature of this relationship in the historical note at Appendix I. The history of the last 150 years has seen two main developments. The first of these has been the gradual restoration to the Church of responsibility for the conduct of its own affairs, although still within the context of the Church's established status and of the legislative supremacy of Parliament.

2.21   The second has been the gradual inclusion of representative clergy and laity in the governing institutions of the Church. In the middle of the nineteenth century the revival of the Convocations restored to the clergy a place in the government of the Church. The Church of England Assembly (Powers) Act 1919 (the 1919 Act) gave to the then Church Assembly delegated legislative power in Church matters. By this legislation, as Archbishop Lang commented, 'For the first time, at least since almost primitive ages, the laity in every parish throughout the land are offered vote and voice in the management of their Church. . . . In a degree never before possible, every man or woman who professes allegiance to the Church is now invested with a personal responsibility for its welfare, for the success or failure of its Divine Mission.'[4]

2.22   The reasons for these developments need to be explicitly acknowledged. They lie, not simply in administrative fashion or convenience but, as the Turnbull Report suggests, in the theology of 'gracious gift' and the inter-relation of the gifts which the Spirit gives to all members of the Body, who do not all have the same function. In particular they provide for those entrusted with oversight to exercise this in relation to the gifts of the whole people of God. For this reason the Church of England provides structures for the bishop to work with his diocese in the diocesan synod, for the collegiality of bishops and also for the college of bishops to act as part of a national synod. ' . . . a synod is one way in which counsel can be taken and consent sought, and the skills and judgement of the whole people of God be brought to bear on the issues and challenges of the day.' (Turnbull Report, 1.19)

2.23   The history of the universal Church shows that there has been no single pattern of ecclesiastical authority. Different periods of history and different ecclesiastical traditions provide examples of how personal, collegial and communal ways of exercising authority have existed in tension and still do. The Church of England is no exception, as is again shown by its history (see Appendix I) and by its continuing to wrestle with this issue in seeking to be obedient to God's will and to be the more effective in its life and mission in His Name.

---

4   Sermon by Archbishop Lang quoted in Eric Waldram Kemp, *Counsel and Consent – Aspects of the Government of the Church as exemplified in the History of English Provincial Synods*, (Bampton Lectures for 1960), SPCK, 1961, page 202.

3

The contemporary context

3.1   In the preceding chapter, we have described the theological principles on which synodical government is founded, and briefly touched on its historical development in England. There is one other building block we need to put in place before we can move to offer our suggestions for synodical government's further development; what is the context – in Church and society – in which synodical government will have to operate both now and in the foreseeable future?

Developments in the Church

3.2   The Church of England is a national Church, with a ministry to all the people of England. The parochial system is the practical manifestation of the Church's continuing commitment to a country-wide ministry.

3.3   Parishes do not, however, exist in isolation. They find their place within the universal Church in their relationship through their bishop with other churches in the locality and with other groupings of local churches beyond it. In this sense it is the diocese not the parish which is the fundamental unit of the universal Church.

3.4   Nevertheless the parish is in many practical senses the basic unit of the Church. Recent developments are serving to underline its fundamental importance:

• as a focus of mission, in the threefold sense of worship, service and witness;

• as both generator and consumer of the great majority of the Church's resources.

The participation of all parishes in synodical government is now even more important than ever.

3.5   One of the purposes of synodical government is to provide an accepted means not only of governing the Church in each place but of helping to mediate its relations with the wider Church beyond that place. If it is to perform this essential mediating function, synodical government must operate in a way which carries the confidence of those in the parishes. The involvement of bishops, clergy and laity in synodical government in the Church of England seeks to emphasise the continuing responsibility of each to all within the Church. The Church of England is and must continue to be a Church in which the local is valued both for itself and as part of the whole Church, in which parish is not set against diocese or province but reaches its fulfilment in relationship to them, and through them to the universal Church.

3.6   The emphasis on the local church as a centre of mission – of which one recent example is Canon Robert Warren's book *Building Missionary Congregations* – reflects a wider shift within the Church as a whole in which mission is seen as the primary focus of the contemporary Church. This is mainly a reaction to the perception that the Gospel message is increasingly at risk of being marginalised in a predominantly secularised or post-modern society, a society which is paradoxically the more in need of that message. The Decade of Evangelism requested by the 1988 Lambeth Conference has resulted in calls for the remodelling of all aspects of the Church's organisation to serve the purposes of mission – for a shift from maintenance to mission.

3.7   Parishes are increasingly responding to these calls but also increasingly irked by the burden, as they see it, of supporting diocesan and national structures – of which the institutions of synodical government are part – which demand their resources but of whose relevance to the Church's mission and ministry they are unsure. Consequent upon the financial challenges confronting the Church they are faced with increasing demands for parish share or quota, which many are having to carry with at best steady levels of active church-goers and overall with a smaller number of clergy to serve them. In these circumstances the generally positive response from parishes to the call for more giving is encouraging. Nevertheless their concerns remain and need to be addressed.

3.8   The renewed emphasis on mission is thus being paralleled by a shift in influence within the Church, as a result of the shift in the burden of financing away from the income from historic resources to the shoulders of the Church in the parishes. This shift will be accelerated by one of the key recommendations in the Turnbull Report – that in future the cost of the Church's national institutions should be wholly or largely borne by the dioceses (and therefore the parishes). This looks likely to give dioceses and parishes even greater say in determining the overall costs of the Church at national level.

3.9   The Turnbull Report is the other key contextual development within the Church itself. The Report's proposal for the establishment of an Archbishops' Council will see the development for the first time of a single focus of policy and resource co-ordination at the national level. This should have significant implications for the inter-relationship between the various national institutions of the Church's government, not least the proposed Council, the House of Bishops and the General Synod.

Developments in society

3.10   Alongside these developments in the Church are various developments in society which set part of the context in which synodical government has to function. It is not our task here to analyse the various changes in society which have been grouped under the label 'post-modernism'.[1] Our point is simply that the institutions of the Church's government have to operate within a social and cultural context which provides a series of expectations, constraints and opportunities. Key features of that context include:

- a high level of uncertainty and unpredictability;

- a rich and varied pluralism of ideas, communities, cultures and faiths;

- a rapidly changing technology, which is revolutionising (among other things) communication and information;

- a cult of individualism coupled with consumer choice;

- great emphasis on the communal ownership of authority, on consent and on accountability.

---

1   For a fuller treatment of these see *Tomorrow is Another Country*, GS Misc 467, Church House Publishing, 1996.

3.11   Some may see these developments as welcome, others as not. Our attitude to them is in one sense, however, irrelevant. The relevant point to our present review is that organisational arrangements in the Church cannot be isolated from the factors which are affecting the discussion and operation of organisational forms in the rest of society.

Developments in organisational theory and practice

3.12   These changes in cultural context are reflected in some of the dominant concepts in current organisational theory. Surveying these briefly, we see some of their key features as being:

- an emphasis on subsidiarity, that is the notion that activities should be carried out at the lowest level at which they can efficiently be undertaken;[2]

- an appreciation of successful organisations as being organic and flexible, constantly open to change and development, with clarity of goals but permeable boundaries and adaptable methods of working;

- a move from uniform, legalistic, rigidly hierarchical organisations to ones which are federal in character, with a clear focus of decision-making but openness and mutual accountability between the parts;

- processes of decision-making which emphasise discussion, openness and consensus.

---

2   The concept of subsidiarity has its classical formulation in an Encyclical letter, *Quadragesimo Anno*, by Pope Pius XII in 1931. Its crucial words are:

> 'it is an injustice, a grave evil and a disturbance of right order for a larger and higher association to arrogate to itself functions which can be performed efficiently by smaller and lower societies.'

Pope Pius saw himself formulating an unchangeable fundamental principle of social philosophy: subsidiarity protects social groupings and their members. The State, this principle argues, risks being distracted by business of minor importance and things which can properly be done better elsewhere. Functions which can be effectively accomplished by smaller groups should be left to them.

The concept was developed as much to protect the individual and family from encroachment by the State as anything else. It has since been applied to many different organisational contexts.

Some criteria for reviewing Church organisation and proposals for its reform

3.13   Many of these features are already to be found in Church government but others are not. What are the tests which we have applied in reviewing synodical government and examining proposals for its reform?

3.14   The key tests which we believe that systems for the overall government of the Church need to meet are:

- they must be true to the theological principles and the Anglican tradition which we discuss in Chapter 2;

- they must take full account of the pattern of historical development which we have described briefly in Chapter 2 and more fully in Appendix I;

- they must seek to build on the major strengths and to remedy the major weaknesses of synodical government as currently perceived;

- they should embody what is both relevant and best in contemporary organisational thinking and fits the context in which the Church finds itself, both now and in the foreseeable future;

- they should be at affordable cost commensurate with the task in terms of both time and money.

3.15   We summarise the key features of the arrangements for the Church's government we seek by saying that they should:

- be as light as possible (so as to minimise the burden of time and money they impose) while being robust enough to stand the various demands on them. They must serve to enable and not disable the mission and ministry of the Church;

- be flexible and adaptable;

- embody principles of subsidiarity;

- foster openness, mutual accountability and trust.

3.16   We now turn to consider in greater detail how well these features are embodied in synodical government as it is presently arranged, and to make proposals for future reform.

4

The parish

4.1   The Turnbull Report says that the significance of the parish system is:

> 'that it is the local, ancient and deeply rooted manifestation of the Church of England's nationwide service, worship and witness. The residents of every parish have the right to attend services, to receive the ministration of the Church and parish clergy, to be married in the parish church and (if space is available) to be buried within the parish. . . . In Christian history it developed together with the office of the bishop, by which care was taken for the continuity and effectiveness of the Christian mission.' (paragraph 2.7)

4.2   It is appropriate therefore that we should begin our examination of synodical government by examining its operation at the level which impacts directly on most people, whether they are active church-goers or not. The evidence we received did not suggest a significant level of dissatisfaction with synodical government at the parish level. There are inevitably some parishes where it works less well than others, but the criticisms are generally of the individuals who use, abuse or are ignorant of the structures rather than of the structures themselves. The apparent general feeling that the system works well at parish level may be due partly to the fact that parochial church councils (PCCs) are a long established feature of Church government, and also in part to the flexibility which is built into the present arrangements allowing individual parishes some freedom in matters such as the size of the council and its ways of working.

4.3   PCCs are essentially local, which means that those most affected by their decisions have relatively easy access to them and, in theory at least, those making the decisions should be aware of the impact they are likely to have.

4.4   Nevertheless, a number of particular points of concern have been drawn to our attention. We examine these in turn below.

The church electoral roll

4.5   The first area of concern involves eligibility to vote and to stand for election to the PCC and other church offices. A particular anxiety expressed in evidence to us was that it is possible under present arrangements for parishioners who rarely attend public worship but who are unhappy about the direction in which an incumbent and the PCC may be moving the church, or who oppose a specific decision, to gain control of the PCC by encouraging their supporters to attend and vote at the annual parochial church meeting. This is to some extent a sign of the democratic nature of the election process at parish level, but it has led to calls for tighter rules about eligibility to be on the church electoral roll.

4.6   It is the entry of a person's name on the church electoral roll of a parish which, for lay people, creates the right and opportunity to participate in the processes of synodical government. The roll is established under the provisions of the Church Representation Rules set out in a schedule to the Synodical Government Measure 1969 (the 1969 Measure). Section 7 of the Measure expressly provides that these rules 'may at any time be amended by a resolution of the General Synod passed by a majority in each House of not less than two thirds of those present and voting.' Any such resolution is however 'subject to annulment in pursuance of a resolution of either House of Parliament.'

4.7   Under Rule 1 (for the text of this rule and other legislative provisions referred to throughout the report, see Appendix III) a lay person who is baptised, aged sixteen or over, a self-declared member of the Church of England or of a Church in communion with the Church of England and who is either resident in the parish or has habitually attended public worship in the parish for six months, is entitled, on application, to have his or her name entered on the church electoral roll.

4.8   The rules do not define what constitutes 'habitual' attendance at public worship. Rule 1 (9) does, however, provide that a person's name shall be removed from the roll if he ceases to reside in the parish unless, after so ceasing, he continues habitually to attend public worship in the parish in any period of six months except when prevented from doing so by illness or other sufficient cause.

4.9   Some who submitted evidence to us argued that a test of 'habitual' attendance at public worship should also apply to those resident in the parish. Others took the view that entitlement to have one's name on the electoral roll should be confined in all circumstances to those who are 'actual communicants.' That expression is defined in Rule 54 (1) as a person who has received Communion according to the use of the Church of England or of a Church in communion with the Church of England at least three times during the twelve months preceding the date of his election or appointment. Those who take the view that the roll should be confined to communicants are usually concerned that eligibility for enrolment should require some defined level of commitment to the Church of England, and to the life of the Church in the parish, together with an acceptance of the implications of such a commitment. Such a provision, it is argued, would also ensure that the membership of the roll reflected more accurately the worshipping community in the parish.

4.10   We have some sympathy with these views. It would mark a sense that entitlement to enrolment carried with it certain responsibilities, and that in order to be able to play an informed part in the government of the Church a person should be able to demonstrate a particular kind and level of commitment to the local church. On the other hand, a narrowing of eligibility in this way would be seen by some as a step towards restricting the Church of England to the active worshipping community and as a weakening of the rights of the ordinary parishioner. We believe that in practice it would be very difficult to secure agreement about what the particular kind and level of required commitment should be and that even if there were such agreement it would be difficult to draft provisions appropriate for inclusion in legislation. We would wish to emphasise that a means of establishing eligibility to vote and seek synodical election (the electoral roll) is not the same thing as a roll of the membership of the Church of England. **We do not therefore recommend any amendment to this aspect of the rules as they are at present.** We do, however, consider that the present provisions governing eligibility for election to the PCC should be tightened. Our recommendations on that point are set out in paragraph 4.14 below.

The PCC

(A)   ELIGIBILITY FOR ELECTION TO THE PCC

4.11   Once a person's name has been entered on the electoral roll he or she has the right to attend and to take part in the annual parochial church meeting (Rule 6 (2)). One of the functions of the annual meeting is to elect representatives of the laity to the PCC.

4.12   Eligibility for election to a PCC as a representative of the laity is governed by Rule 10 (1), which provides that the person must have his name entered on the roll of the parish, be at least 16 years old and be 'an actual communicant.' As we have indicated earlier, this phrase is defined in Rule 54 (1) as a person who has received Communion according to the use of the Church of England or of a Church in communion with the Church of England at least three times during the twelve months preceding the date of his election or appointment.

4.13   We believe that candidates for election to a PCC should have demonstrated a regular pattern of worship in the parish over a period of time – a year at least – and that this should be more than simply complying with the definition of an 'actual communicant.' However, it is one thing to say this; it is another to embody it in legal rules. For example, it would not be appropriate, in our view, to attempt to specify a minimum number of church attendances as a specific legal requirement.

4.14   **We do recommend however that provision should be included in Rule 10 (1) that candidates shall not be eligible for election to a PCC unless their names have been on the electoral roll for a period of at least twelve months.** In that period the candidate will have been able to demonstrate his or her commitment to the life, worship and witness of the parish. The date of enrolment is easily ascertained. Such a provision would not preclude the PCC from using its power to co-opt a person whose name had recently been entered on the electoral roll, if in all the circumstances it thought it appropriate to do so.

(B)   PCC MEMBERS' TERM OF OFFICE

4.15   Under the present Rule 16 (1) elected lay members of the PCC hold office from one annual meeting to the next. But there is a proviso to the rule which allows the annual meeting to decide, in effect, that lay members shall be elected for a three year term and that one-third of them shall retire annually in rotation. We think this makes for better continuity in the work of the PCC and should be prescribed by the rules for all PCCs.

4.16   **We recommend that Rule 16 (1) be amended so that the system of election under the proviso, which now only operates if the annual meeting so decides, be prescribed for all PCCs, with the effect that lay members will be elected for a three year term and one-third of them will retire annually in rotation but be eligible for re-election.**

4.17   We received evidence to the effect that, on rare occasions when there is disagreement in a parish, one faction or the other may come to the annual parochial church meeting in force to elect those of their persuasion on to the PCC. If our recommendation about one-third only of the PCC retiring each year is implemented, this would mean that while scope for flexible change would still be provided, it would not be possible for a faction in a parish wholly to 'take over' the PCC at a single annual meeting.

4.18   Another refinement in PCC elections in the existing rules is a discretionary provision which enables the annual meeting to decide that, after a specific number of consecutive periods of three years, a person should be ineligible for further election until after a break of, say, one year. We consider that it should continue to be a matter for decision by the annual parochial church meeting whether or not to activate this provision.

(C)   CONSTITUTION OF THE PCC

4.19   The membership of a PCC is governed by Rule 14 (see Appendix III.2). The incumbent, any other clergy, deaconesses and lay workers licensed to the parish, members of a team ministry serving the parish and the churchwardens are all members ex-officio, as are also persons whose names are on the roll of the parish and who are lay members of any deanery synod, diocesan synod or the General Synod. Lay readers in the parish are ex-officio members only if the annual parochial church meeting so decides. The number of elected lay members is also as decided by the annual meeting, any alteration taking effect at the ensuing annual meeting. There is also a limited power of co-option. The evidence before us and our own deliberations led us to consider possible changes in PCC membership in only three respects, namely in relation to the number of elected lay members, to licensed lay readers and to retired clergy.

(D)   SIZE OF THE PCC

4.20   Some of the representations we received expressed concern that some PCCs were over-large. At present the annual meeting is free to determine the number of lay representatives to be elected to the PCC under Rule 14 (1) (g). We think that, in principle, this is right; it enables each parish to decide the size of council best suited to its needs. We are aware, however, that the size of councils can vary widely and can go un-reviewed for many years. We therefore take the view that the present rule should be amended to provide defined parameters as a norm, with the annual meeting remaining free nevertheless to make a different specific determination if it believes it right to do so.

4.21   **Accordingly we recommend that the rule should be amended to provide that, unless the annual parochial meeting determines otherwise, the number of lay representatives to be elected to the PCC should be nine plus three additional representatives for each 100 members (or part thereof) on the electoral roll over 100.** Thus the statutory norm would be followed unless a specific decision were taken by the annual meeting to make a different provision. In the light of our recommendation in paragraph 4.16 above that one-third of the elected lay representatives of the PCC should retire each year (subject to a right to stand for immediate re-election), the numbers to be elected should be multiples of three.

(E)   Categories of membership of the PCC

4.22   Turning to the categories of membership of the PCC, we received no suggestions for change to the provisions in relation to beneficed or licensed clergy or to churchwardens in sections (a), (b), (c) or (d) set out in Appendix III.2.

4.23   With regard to category (e) – licensed lay readers – it was represented to us that the provisions should be amended so as to provide that at least one reader in any parish should have ex-officio membership of the PCC. At one time the annual meeting could determine that either all readers whose names were on the electoral roll should be ex-officio PCC members or that none should be. The Elections Review Group (which advises the General Synod on amendments to the rules) received expressions of concern that in some parishes there were a large number of readers who thereby had membership and, it was argued, as a result the PCC became unbalanced. That Group therefore proposed to the General Synod, and the Synod accepted, that each parish should decide for itself whether and, if so, how many, readers should have ex-officio membership. The rules were amended to this effect in 1973. In 1995 a further qualification was added by confining the category to readers 'licensed to that parish or licensed to an area which includes that parish.'

4.24   We have considered this matter again. It may well be appropriate that there should be a reader on the PCC. But we have to ask why special provision should be made for readers and not for pastoral assistants or other types of authorised lay ministers. Like other communicants on the electoral roll, readers are entitled to seek election to the PCC and may also be co-opted to it. We believe it appropriate that the annual meeting of the parish should decide, in the light of its own circumstances, whether a reader or readers should have ex-officio membership of the PCC as an addition to, or as an alternative to, readers standing for election alongside other parishioners. **We therefore recommend no change to the rule.**

4.25   We return in the next chapter to the provisions of category (f) in Appendix III.2 concerning the inclusion in the membership of the PCC of the lay members of the deanery synod. We see positive advantage in the provisions of that section concerning ex-officio membership for diocesan synod members and General Synod members. Such members are then involved in the running of the church at parochial level. In our view this is essential if they are to discharge their responsibilities most effectively because it ensures they are kept in touch with grass roots opinion. **We therefore recommend no change to the rule.**

4.26   Some concern was expressed to us that under the present rules retired clergy who had the bishop's permission to officiate rather than his licence were neither ex-officio members of the PCC nor were eligible for election to it. We recognise that there can be circumstances in which it may well be appropriate for such clergy to be members of the PCC. However we do not believe that the rules should themselves make specific provision in this regard. Rather we think it more appropriate that the PCC should consider, in appropriate circumstances, exercising the power of co-option which it has under section (h) of the present rule.

4.27   The power of co-option in category (h) is a useful tool for a PCC to have to help ensure that it has access to all the skills and experience it requires. **We do not recommend any change.**

(F)   THE FUNCTIONS OF A PCC

4.28   A number of the functions of a PCC are set out in the PCC (Powers) Measure 1956 (see Appendix III.3). Others are to be found in other Measures which have been passed by the Church Assembly and the Synod over the years. In the main, they can be summarised by saying that the purpose of the PCC is to provide a means through which the incumbent and the other members of the council can consult together on matters of general concern and importance to the parish, including the effective discharge of their respective responsibilities. In particular, the 1956 Measure requires the PCC to co-operate with the incumbent in promoting in the parish the whole mission of the Church, pastoral, evangelistic, social and ecumenical.

4.29   **Subject to the changes consequent upon the recommendations we make in Chapter 5 concerning deanery synods, we do not think it is necessary to propose amendments to the prescribed functions of a PCC.**

(G)   THE CHAIRMANSHIP OF THE PCC

4.30   The initial assumption under the Church Representation Rules was that the incumbent or priest in charge should chair meetings of the PCC, with the vice-chairman (who must be a lay member of the PCC) taking the chair in his absence (see Appendix III.4). At the last revision of the rules this requirement was relaxed to some extent by the inclusion of a provision to the effect that the chairman presiding may vacate the chair either generally or for a specific item of business. The rules already provide that at a meeting the PCC can resolve that the chairman vacate the chair. We received evidence that clergy are no more guaranteed to make good chairmen than laity, and it was argued that the rule should be amended so that there is no automatic right for the parish priest to chair the PCC, but that each PCC should be free to choose from among its members the person (whether clergy or lay) best suited to this task.

4.31   We are conscious that some clergy would see such a change as a diminution of their role and feel that they were being disadvantaged in the care and leadership of the parish. It has to be remembered that it is the chairman of the PCC who has power to call meetings of the council, including emergency meetings called at short notice, and who, if votes are equally divided, has the casting vote (see Appendix III.4). In most parishes the chairman is consulted by the secretary about the content of the PCC agenda.

4.32   We consider that the present provisions relating to chairmanship of the PCC provide all the flexibility that is needed. **We recommend no change.**

District Church Councils (DCCs): Joint Church Councils (JCCs)

4.33   By virtue of section 3 of the Parochial Church Councils (Powers) Measure 1956 a PCC is a body corporate and has perpetual succession. In the last thirty years a number of other bodies have been created either by the Pastoral Measure or by the Church Representation Rules, namely DCCs, JCCs, team councils and group councils. It was suggested to us in evidence that DCCs, and JCCs in particular, should, by Measure, be corporate bodies. The reasons for this suggestion seem to be twofold. If the bodies in question are not incorporated, it is argued, first, that this calls into question their charitable status, and, secondly, that there could be legal liability falling on the individual members of such councils for their collective actions.

4.34   The Legal Advisory Commission of the General Synod gave an opinion in 1990 that the Pastoral Measure 1983 (Schedule 3, paragraph 13) does not provide for the incorporation of JCCs because this is not specifically referred to in the Measure nor in section 3 of the 1956 Measure which is attracted by paragraph 13. There is an additional point that the Measure only provides for a limited life of five years for such councils unless they are reactivated by the annual meeting. We were also advised that the General Synod's Elections Review Group has considered this point and concluded that a proliferation of corporate bodies would add unnecessary complication to this aspect of the law of the Church. We see force in this argument. In addition, enhancing the legal status of DCCs would in our view be contrary to the spirit of collaborative ministry, especially where a team has been created.

4.35   Where a DCC works to the PCC, the PCC will continue to be the corporate body having charitable status and thus protecting individual council members from legal liability for a debt of the PCC or the DCC (for example). If a DCC attempts to run its affairs as an independent body, the members of the DCC may well be exposed to legal liability for their actions. It would also probably expose the PCC to liability, it being the corporate body, were the PCC to permit such a situation to develop.

4.36   There is no legal doubt with regard to the charitable status of the PCC. The new Charities Act Accounting Regulations will also make it clear that the PCC is the responsible unit in respect of the accounts of the parish. If more autonomy is thought appropriate for a district, in our view, the solution is to form the district into a separate parish with its own PCC; if there are a number of districts in the same area to be formed into parishes, consideration could be given to having a JCC for the team.

4.37   JCCs are sometimes brought into being under the Church Representation Rules to enable parishes which remain distinct to work more closely together in those areas where the parishes concerned deem it appropriate. We see JCCs as a useful device in the process of bringing parishes closer together but, in our view, establishing JCCs as separate corporate bodies might ossify that process rather than being a means of achieving the appropriate goal which, in suitable cases, might be a union of parishes.

4.38   For similar reasons we do not see it as appropriate that team councils or group councils should be incorporated.

Conventional districts

4.39   The conventional district is an anomaly at parish level. The conventional district is not a parish, but is an area placed under the care of a priest in charge by agreement between the incumbent(s) of the parish(es) in which the district is situated and the bishop. The agreement must be renewed with every change of incumbency. The priest in charge is responsible for those living in the district. Such districts are usually to be found in new housing areas and are formed with a view to their subsequently becoming distinct parishes. In the Pastoral Measure 1983 the definition of 'parish' does not include a conventional district, but in the Church Representation Rules 'parish' does include a conventional district. Consequently a conventional district can have churchwardens, and may have its own parochial church council separate from that of the parishes to which it belongs. This understandably causes confusion. **We therefore recommend that conventional districts should be removed from the definition of 'parish' in the Church Representation Rules.**

4.40   We make this recommendation because, in our view, when such a district is formed a district church council should be constituted with deputy churchwardens: this is possible under Rule 18. We would see this as better highlighting the transitional nature of the district and encouraging those in the district to move on to full parochial status at the appropriate time. Under the present law, because a conventional district already has its own PCC and churchwardens, there is some evidence that those locally see no necessity to move on to the creation of a separate parish, and one or two conventional districts are still in existence forty years after their creation. **We recommend that in any conventional district, in addition to a renewal of the agreement with every change of incumbency, there should also be a review of the pastoral situation by the bishop and the diocesan pastoral committee at five yearly intervals.**

The human element

4.41   In the preceding paragraphs we have focused on particular structural questions raised in evidence put to us. As we noted at the outset of this chapter, however, when problems arise in the operation of synodical government at the parish level it is frequently a result not of deficiencies in the system but of deficiencies in the way people use it. This is not a problem unique to the parochial level.

4.42   In the closing sentences of this chapter we wish to emphasise the desirability of educating and training those who hold positions of authority in the Church at parish level in the principles and good practice of synodical government. We are not suggesting elaborate new programmes but we are aware of how valuable it is for ordinands, clergy and laity to understand why the system of synodical government in the Church of England has developed as it has, and of the spirit in which it is to be conducted. We are also aware of how useful diocesan or deanery training days can be in teaching practical skills such as chairing meetings or on being a churchwarden or parish treasurer.

4.43   We end this chapter with a tribute to all those involved in the running of PCCs, both ordained and lay. We are all aware from first-hand experience of the many hours of selfless work which go into the various aspects of running a parish, of which the PCC is one. It is a tribute to all involved that so few complaints about the operation of synodical government at the parish level were made to us.

5

The deanery

5.1   Of the four tiers of synodical government (PCC, deanery, diocesan and General Synods), it is the deanery synod which attracted most attention in the evidence submitted to us. There was general acceptance of the need for the national Church to have some form of national representative assembly although there are many views about its size and functions. At diocesan level the need for a consultative and decision-making body was also recognised. At parish level too there was little doubt that local churches needed some form of council or committee to function effectively. However, about deanery synods (as distinct from deaneries) there was far more doubt. In this chapter we make recommendations about the deanery synod in the light of these reservations. We emphasise at the outset however that our recommendations are not intended to call into question the future of the deanery as a geographical unit for mission, administration and pastoral care. It is on the deanery synod that we focus.

5.2   The evidence we received suggested that it was very difficult to justify the existence of the deanery synod in its present statutory form. Some, though not many, argued that there was no need at all for deaneries as a geographical unit. Much more concern was expressed however that the deanery synod was ineffective. Archdeaconries, it was pointed out, functioned without the need for 'archdeaconry synods.'

5.3   Nevertheless some affirmed the deanery synod as an effective focus for mission, a forum for consultation between neighbouring parishes and a means of enhancing Christian fellowship and allocating resources. Their success depends, it was argued, on the willingness of parishes to work together, and on the individual initiative and leadership shown, in particular, by the rural dean and the lay chairman.

5.4   During our visits to dioceses we found a wide variation in the responses to our enquiries about deanery synods. There are people at both ends of the spectrum and they each hold their opposing views with great conviction. On the one hand some made a clear call for the abolition of deanery synods. On the other hand there were those who saw the deanery as a crucial link in the structure of the Church and deanery synods as vital to the Church's life and mission.

5.5   In this and the following paragraphs we summarise the criticisms directed at deanery synods. Chief among them is that in many deaneries the synod is perceived as having little relevance to the life of the Church. It is consequently difficult to persuade people to stand for election, and lay membership of the synod tends to become a matter of 'Buggins' turn,' with members having little interest in developing the synod's potential for effective work.

5.6   The broad spectrum of functions allocated to deanery synods by the 1969 Measure (see Appendix III.5) is unrealistic and in practice many of the statutory functions are often simply not performed. Thus, for example, the deanery synod which is effective in promoting in the deanery 'the whole mission of the Church, pastoral, evangelistic, social and ecumenical' is the exception rather than the rule.

5.7   The great variation in size and character of deaneries, many of which appear to have arbitrary boundaries, makes it inappropriate to impose any uniform pattern of synodical government on them. This is reflected in the significant differences in the nature and extent of responsibilities delegated to deanery synods by dioceses.

5.8   In some deaneries the relationship between the clergy chapter and the deanery synod is a source of difficulty. The clergy chapter controls the deanery synod and its agenda. While the laity outnumber the clergy in the synod, on many issues the clergy are better informed and have a greater degree of interest than the laity. The fact that the clerical members meet separately in chapter (for whom it may play an important role in professional support and development) and the laity usually do not meet together separately may enable the clergy to control the direction of the synod. The difficulty of balancing clerical and lay interests is seen clearly in the roles of the rural dean and the lay chairman. In practice it is the rural dean who often has more opportunity to be in touch with the deanery, and who tends to be the person to whom deanery problems are referred – not least because it is the rural dean who is usually more readily available.

5.9 The opportunity for ecumenical initiative in deaneries has been enhanced by the recent changes to the Church Representation Rules which have made it possible for non-Anglicans to play a part in deanery synods. In many places, however, an ecumenical Council of Churches can be a more effective way of promoting joint action and where such councils exist the rationale for a separate Anglican body is weakened. In this situation the deanery synod is sometimes seen as virtually redundant.

5.10 The present arrangements for parish representation on deanery synods are unsatisfactory. The deanery synod is made up proportionately of representatives from every parish in the deanery. But the effect of this on parishes which are united to form a single parish within the same benefice is substantially to reduce their representation. A benefice made up of four separate parishes may have eight or more members on the deanery synod, whilst a neighbouring benefice with the same number of churches but which comprises a single parish may have only two. On major issues this difference in representation can be decisive.

5.11 The lay members of the deanery synod form the electorate for elections to the houses of laity of the diocesan synod and of the General Synod. The difficulties referred to above are also reflected here. A benefice comprising several separate parishes will have more voters in a General Synod election than a single parish with the same number of parishioners and churches. But there are also much wider questions of principle to be addressed. We deal with the question of the base for election to diocesan synods and to the General Synod in Chapter 10.

5.12 Before we offer our own view on these criticisms, it is appropriate to set out something of the history and development of rural deans and rural deaneries.

Rural deans and deaneries

5.13 The office of rural dean is very ancient. It is first recorded in one of the laws ascribed to Edward the Confessor. The rural dean was appointed by the bishop 'to have the inspection of clergy and people within the district in which he was incumbent . . . to which

31

end [he] had power to convene rural chapters.'[1] These chapters were made up of all the instituted clergy, or their curates as proxies for them, with the dean as president.

5.14   By the fifteenth century the jurisdiction of the rural dean had declined to almost nothing as a result of the development of the office of archdeacon. However, by the middle of the last century rural deaneries had been established by statute and the Ecclesiastical Commissioners had power to alter the area of rural deaneries, to increase or diminish their number and to name new ones.[2] The same statute also provided that every parish was in its entirety to be within a rural deanery and since then a number of statutes have given specific powers to the rural dean.

5.15   There are no statutory qualifications for the office of rural dean. Canon C 23 (promulged in 1969) sets out certain of the duties of rural dean. The rural dean is, for example, to report to the bishop any matter in any parish within the deanery 'which it may be necessary or useful for the bishop to know.' He is to inspect the churches in the deanery when this is not carried out by the archdeacon (Canon F 18) and if there is any serious defect in the fabric, ornaments and furniture of any church to report the matter to the archdeacon (Canon C 23). The rural dean is also joint chairman (with a member of the house of laity) of the deanery synod.

Membership of the deanery synod

5.16   The membership of a deanery synod is governed by Rule 24 of the Church Representation Rules (see Appendix III.6). The clerical members comprise all clergy beneficed in or licensed to any parish in the deanery, members of the General Synod or diocesan synod resident in the deanery, certain clergy holding the bishop's licence to work in the deanery and elected representatives of the retired clergy resident in the parish. The lay members comprise the representatives elected by the annual meetings of the parishes in the deanery, members of the General Synod or any diocesan synod whose names are on the roll of any parish in the deanery and deaconesses and lay workers licensed

---

1   *Phillimore's Ecclesiastical Law*, 2nd edition (1895), vol. 1, p. 208

2   37 & 38 Vict. c 62 sec 1.

to work in the deanery. The number of lay representatives to be elected by each parish is as determined by the diocesan synod proportionately to the number of names on the electoral roll, subject to Rule 25 which prescribes 50 and 150 as the normal minimum and maximum number of members for a deanery synod. The synod also has a limited power of co-option.

Proposals for change

5.17   In paragraphs 5.2 to 5.11 above we have set out the concerns expressed to us about the operation of deanery synods. We are quite clear that the deanery continues to be a useful level in the Church, intermediate between diocese and parish, for certain purposes and we believe there must continue to be means through which parishes can be encouraged and enabled to consult and work together and to relate to and be consulted by the diocese as a whole. We see the purposes of the deanery as including arrangements for:

- bringing together representatives of the parishes and providing a focal point for the discussion of common issues;

- being the means of helping parishes to decide how best to minister to the needs of a particular locality;

- being a means of mutual support and encouragement;

- undertaking certain tasks given to it either by the diocese or by parishes.

The deanery can be an effective focus for consultation, for providing information, for liaison between parishes in matters of common concern and, if the relevant power is delegated to it by the diocese, for allocating quota among the constituent parishes and advising on the deployment of clergy within the deanery.

5.18   We have serious doubts, however, whether the present deanery synod as defined by statute is the best means by which these desirable purposes of the deanery can be met. We have come to the view that the establishment of deanery synods with functions and membership prescribed by statute is not a sufficiently flexible way in which to enable and encourage parishes to work together in mission, evangelism and pastoral care. Deaneries need to be freed from the structure, though not the principles, of the synodical system if they are to carry out their role more effectively.

5.19 **We recommend that the statutory requirement for deanery synods to be part of the formal structure of synodical government should be repealed.** In proposing the removal of deaneries from the legislative framework of synodical government, we are not rejecting the idea or importance of deaneries, either in terms of their carrying out responsibilities on behalf of the diocese or as local units of collaborative mission and ministry. We believe it to be more appropriate that each diocese should be free to establish, after consultation with the parishes, local assemblies for consultation and action on shared issues which best suit the particular circumstances of the diocese and deanery. We do not seek to prescribe what these assemblies might be. The dioceses should, we believe, have the flexibility to establish particular schemes for consultation, advice or decision-making which would release the skills and energies available within the parishes for addressing together particular tasks.

5.20 **We recommend each diocese should be required to produce a scheme or schemes for deanery arrangements, to be approved by the diocesan synod, and which should be subject to review every five years.** As we have said, we believe that it would be wrong to prescribe these nationally but that they should reflect local preference and needs. However, we suggest that they should be based on a number of principles. In particular they should:

- provide the opportunity for both clergy and laity to share in the shaping of deanery strategy and activity;

- provide for the election of a lay chairman who will exercise lay leadership alongside the rural dean;

- ensure that both rural dean and lay chairman are recognised by the diocese for consultation and communication purposes;

- clearly define the functions which the diocese will expect to see carried out by the deaneries; and

- provide for consultation on pastoral organisation at deanery level.

5.21   We further recommend that the diocesan determination of deanery arrangements should be strengthened by the repeal of the present provisions in the Pastoral Measure 1983 which require a pastoral scheme or order to be made by the Church Commissioners before a deanery boundary can be altered and the enactment of provisions allowing the primary decision with respect to the alteration of deanery boundaries by the re-allocation of parishes within deaneries to be made by the diocesan synod so as to effect the grouping of parishes most suitable to local needs. If this recommendation is accepted it will be necessary to provide a right for any parish objecting to a re-allocation proposed by the diocese to appeal to some independent body.

5.22   So far as the functions of deaneries are concerned, we see these best being determined at diocesan and deanery levels. Dioceses will want to use deaneries for a variety of purposes, not least as they have regard to the principle of subsidiarity. This may include using them as a channel for communication, the constituency from which membership of diocesan boards and committees is drawn, or as the mechanism through which the apportionment of quota / parish share is determined.

5.23   Deaneries themselves will have their own local agendas, to do with mission and ministry and the support of local church life. This might include shared evangelism, education programmes, training for Sunday school and youth leaders and other such ministries, support for churchwardens, treasurers or church musicians, publication of a joint magazine, etc.

5.24   We are clear that deaneries will require schemes for their effective operation, but again we see this to be a matter to be agreed by each diocese. Different schemes may be appropriate for different deaneries within the same diocese. We see a wide range of possibilities:

*   a council composed in the same way as the current synod. If dioceses want to keep some or all of their current deanery synods because they work for particular deaneries, we do not think they should be denied the opportunity but nor should they be required by statute to do so;

- a smaller body of representatives elected by parishes (nearer to a standing committee in size);

- an annual meeting of parish representatives;

- an annual meeting of such representatives electing an executive or standing committee; or

- a meeting of churchwardens or of other appropriate parish officers.

5.25   We would expect such arrangements to be supplemented by a wide range of less formal means – either Anglican or ecumenical in nature – which would bring relevant people together to tackle particular issues or to oversee particular programmes or activities. Such informal arrangements would reflect and go beyond the present rich variety of ways of working. It would be for deaneries themselves to organise such matters in ways which best suited their own needs, although it would no doubt be useful for the diocese to promote exemplars and disseminate good practice.

5.26   Some may object that our proposals will deprive parishes of an effective say in the affairs of the diocese. We do not accept this. First, we are not convinced that deanery synods provide such a mechanism at present. Secondly, we have suggested alternative structures for consultation and debate which we believe could prove more effective than present arrangements. Thirdly, we regard it as essential that dioceses should, as part of their deanery schemes, ensure means whereby motions from PCCs can be considered by the bishop's council and, if appropriate, the diocesan synod. Our recommendations for new arrangements for the election of lay members to the diocesan synod and to the General Synod (which we discuss in Chapter 10) will also, we believe, strengthen the identification of parishes with the diocese and the General Synod.

6

The diocese

6.1   'Mysterious and irrelevant' is how one correspondent described the diocesan synod. But others see it as 'effective, useful and necessary'. Here again the size and character of the diocese has some bearing on the effectiveness of its diocesan synod. Some see diocesan synods as expensive talking shops which do little more than provide a forum for the diocesan bishop or even for individual members with a particular axe to grind. Others claim that the synod can be an effective body for expressing views on church matters, determining policy and, through its standing committee, for co-ordinating the work of the diocese.

6.2   A number of submissions to us and our own visits to dioceses revealed that the relationships which the diocesan synod has with other bodies, especially the bishop's council and bishop's senior staff, are a crucial factor in its effectiveness. There is apparently a feeling in some dioceses that the synod can do little more than rubber stamp decisions already made elsewhere. In some we have encountered the view that, in reality, the bishop's staff meeting controls both the bishop's council and the synod.

6.3   Questions have been raised with us about the limited opportunities for real debate at diocesan synods. In many cases the synod meetings are taken up with addresses and presentations from diocesan boards or other central bodies, and opportunities for deanery representatives to make their views known are somewhat restricted. In some quarters there is still a desire for the old diocesan conference at which every parish was represented, but most recognise that in all but a few dioceses such a meeting would be too large and likely to be ineffective. There is already provision in the 1969 Measure for the diocesan bishop to summon such a conference of persons appearing to him to be representative of the clergy and laity of the diocese, in addition to diocesan synod meetings, if he so wishes (section 4 (7)).

6.4   Generalisation is difficult. The synod in a large diocese is likely to have a quite different character from that in a small one. The tasks which diocesan synods are asked to undertake also vary considerably. For example, one interesting development in recent years has been the practice of establishing common membership between the diocesan synod and the diocesan board of finance (DBF).

The functions of the diocesan synod

6.5   A number of changes to the present statutory functions of a diocesan synod (for which see Appendix III.7) will be necessary if our proposals in Chapter 5 concerning deanery synods are accepted. Section 4 (5) of the 1969 Measure in particular will need substantial recasting. Arrangements will still be needed for the diocesan synod to hear from and report to parishes and deaneries, and diocesan synods will have to be put under a duty to approve schemes, developed in consultation with parishes, for the effective operation of deaneries. We also believe that the description of the functions of a diocesan synod should be amended to include reference to the role of the synod in receiving the annual accounts and approving the budget for the diocese.

6.6   **For these reasons we recommend there should be added to the statutory functions of a diocesan synod the following:**

(i)   **to approve the annual budget and to receive the annual accounts for the diocese;**

(ii)   **to approve schemes for the effective operation of deaneries;**

(iii) **to keep deaneries and parishes informed of the policies and problems of the diocese, of the issues the diocesan synod is to consider and of the decisions it takes, and to receive and, where necessary, to take action on matters referred to it from deaneries and parishes.**

The membership and size of the diocesan synod

6.7   A further consequence of the recommendations we have made about deanery synods in Chapter 5 is that there will need to be established a different electorate for the election of the members of the house of laity of diocesan synods (and of the General Synod). Our recommendations on this are contained in Chapter 10.

6.8 We received representations from the Retired Clergy Association that retired clergy who had a permission to officiate from the bishop (rather than a licence) should also be eligible to stand for election to diocesan synods (and to the General Synod). This is also a matter we discuss in Chapter 10.

6.9 As we have already indicated, the size of a diocesan synod is a matter which was also raised in evidence to us. At present, under Rule 31 (6) of the Church Representation Rules, the diocesan synod determines the number of members to be elected to it by deanery synods. However, under Rule 31 (8) the diocesan synod is required to exercise that determination so as to secure that the 'number of members of the Synod is not less than 150 and not more than 270 and that the numbers of members of the houses of clergy and laity are approximately equal.'

6.10 We take the view that the numbers of members of the houses of clergy and laity of diocesan synods should indeed continue to be approximately equal. We have considered whether to recommend that the prescribed minimum of 150 and maximum of 270 should be amended. We concluded that it was right that the provisions of Rule 31 (8) should be amended to provide that the presently prescribed minimum number of members of a diocesan synod should be 100 rather than 150. We saw no case however for proposing that the maximum number should be either increased or reduced from the presently prescribed maximum of 270. Rather we think it right that within the wider parameters provided by the reduction of the prescribed minimum to 100, dioceses should have discretion to set the size of their diocesan synod to suit their own circumstances. **We recommend therefore that Rule 31 (8) be amended to provide that the minimum number of members of a diocesan synod should be 100, and that each diocese should review the size of its diocesan synod, taking account of the reality of the falling numbers of clergy, and of laity registered on the electoral rolls of parishes.**

Bishop's council and standing committee of the diocesan synod

6.11   Section 4 (4) of the 1969 Measure provides that 'the advisory and consultative functions of the diocesan synod . . . may be discharged . . . by the bishop's council and standing committee.' Since 1970 the bishop's council has played an increasingly significant role in the life of the diocese. Indeed a report from one diocese described the council as being 'at the heart of diocesan life.' Certainly the evidence presented to us suggested that it performs a vital part in the making of policy at diocesan level.

6.12   In the 1969 model standing orders for diocesan synods (which do not have statutory force), the functions of the bishop's council are set out as:

(i)   to plan the business of the synod, to prepare the agenda for its sessions, and to circulate to members information about matters for discussion;

(ii)   to initiate proposals for action by the synod and to advise it on matters of policy which are placed before it;

(iii)   to advise the president on any matters which he may refer to the committee;

(iv)   subject to the directions of the synod to transact the business of the synod when not in session;

(v)   to appoint members of committees or nominate members for election to committees, subject to the directions of the synod;

(vi)   to carry out such other functions as the synod may delegate to it.

6.13   The model standing orders suggest that the membership of the bishop's council should be the president (i.e. the diocesan bishop), the vice presidents (i.e. the chairmen of the houses of clergy and laity of the diocesan synod), all other members of the house of bishops, the archdeacons, the chairman of the DBF and a group of elected members ordained and lay. In 1990 the Elections Review Group suggested that the elected members be such that the total membership of the council is not more than 25, nor less than 15; that every archdeaconry in the diocese has at least one clerical and one lay representative elected by

40

the members of the diocesan synod who represent that archdeaconry in their respective houses; that the number of elected members exceeds the ex-officio members by at least 50 per cent; and that as far as possible the number of clerical and lay members of the council, including ex-officio membership, is equal. However, the only present statutory provision concerning the membership of the bishop's council is Rule 34 of the Church Representation Rules (Procedure for Diocesan Synods). This provides 'that there shall be a bishop's council and standing committee of the diocesan synod with such membership as may be provided by standing orders.'

6.14   Whilst we received some evidence critical of both the concept and the working of the bishop's council (mainly on the apparently contradictory grounds either that it had too much power or that it was ineffective), there was little evidence of significant dissatisfaction. Indeed there were those who expressed the opinion that since, in their view, the diocesan synod was little more than a rubber stamp for decisions reached elsewhere, the council should replace the diocesan synod in the interests of effectiveness and financial saving. They suggested an increase in the membership of the council by the inclusion in it of rural deans and lay chairmen of deanery synods together with the diocesan members of the General Synod. We do not accept this argument. We suspect that to augment the council in this way would damage its effectiveness as an executive body while not satisfying the demand of the parishes for representation at the diocesan level. **We therefore recommend that it should remain a matter for the diocesan synod to determine the size of its bishop's council and that this should not be prescribed by legislation.**

6.15   However, our visits to dioceses did reveal two areas of concern about the ability of the bishop's council to discharge its desired function of long-term planning for the diocese. The first of these lies in the separation between policy-making and decisions about the collecting and allocating of resources which is reflected in the separate existence of the bishop's council and the DBF. There is ample evidence of the wish of many dioceses to change this situation. Some have already gone ahead and have made the diocesan synod the DBF and the bishop's council its executive. We comment further on this in paragraphs 6.24 et seq. below.

6.16   The other area of concern is a particularly sensitive one and involves the relationship of the bishop's senior staff meeting to the bishop's council. There appears to be a widespread feeling that the senior staff meeting is where key policy decisions affecting the diocese are taken. The question of who attends meetings of his senior staff is entirely a matter for the diocesan bishop; the general pattern is, however, that suffragan bishops, archdeacons, and the dean or provost attend, as does the diocesan secretary. In some cases, or for particular items, others too may be invited. The fact that its members are full-timers, at the heart of the diocese, and therefore have more knowledge of the needs and possibilities of the diocese, is assumed to mean that the meeting must – in some sense – dominate diocesan policy, thus diminishing the status and role of the bishop's council as the representative executive body under the diocesan synod.

6.17   We suspect that part of the problem might be the mystery which surrounds the senior staff meeting. Through the Bishop of Blackburn we therefore enquired of eleven diocesan bishops about their use of the staff meeting. A remarkably uniform picture emerged, with agendas which concentrated on pastoral matters, appointments and information exchange – supported by prayer and theological reflection (see the specimen agenda at Appendix III.9). This matches the definition given to us by Lord Habgood, the former Archbishop of York, who saw the consideration of diocesan policy as a matter for the bishop's council and the principal tasks of the staff meeting as being concerned with pastoral (and therefore often confidential) matters, patronage and appointments, and with providing an opportunity for the diocesan staff to keep abreast with what is going on.

6.18   While each bishop and diocese will find their own pattern, we believe that the primary role for the staff meeting is the pastoral one we have described. It will be part of reality that the staff meeting will also be the place where the bishop, with his senior colleagues, can work up ideas and develop leadership. It should equally be part of reality that the bishop uses his council, and through it the synod, to encourage reflection, to consult, to secure support for leadership and to develop diocesan strategy and policy, and shape the way in which resources – both of money and people – are used to further the ministry and mission of the Church.

6.19   This issue brings us near to the heart of the episcopal–synodical relationship. The decision-making role on policy and resources lies with the diocesan synod, but the bishop, exercising his leadership role through his council, will be a major influence in the synod as together they shape the ministry and mission of the diocese.

6.20   The style of leadership, gifts and personality of the diocesan bishop will be central to what happens in practice in the relationship between him, his staff, his council and the synod. We urge bishops to be sensitive to the proper concerns of the council and to give it the opportunity to play a full role in the diocese.

6.21   If the council is to play a full and creative part, membership of the bishop's council must be taken seriously. We received some evidence that what it means (and demands) to be a member is not always properly understood; of some members failing to give sufficient energy and commitment; and of members being unable to reflect theologically or unwilling to think deeply – or not being helped to do so. We hope for a better understanding both of the role of the council and of what it means to be a member of it in the future. To this end we encourage the development within dioceses of greater clarity of expectations and responsibilities, and the provision of opportunities to equip members to be clear about their role and responsibilities through appropriate induction and training.

6.22   Under existing law the bishop's council and synod standing committee are combined, though in practice the latter role is often undertaken by a sub-group. We suspect that the more weight that is put on the bishop's council as advisory and consultative to the bishop, the more important it will be that some members should be suitably qualified for that role while others will need the quite different capacity for business management called for from the members of a standing committee. These diverse qualifications may be best secured by appointment (or a combination of appointment and election) of the members to the council rather than by election alone.

6.23   We see these as issues which require careful thought and determination locally, and not as matters for national prescription. They are similar to issues which are part of the debate at national level about follow-up to the Turnbull Report, in particular, about the membership of the proposed Archbishops' Council. **We recommend** that dioceses should be encouraged to review their arrangements for membership of their bishop's council in the light of whatever pattern emerges at the national level.

Diocesan infrastructure

6.24   In its chapter on the dioceses, the Turnbull Report says:

> '10.10 Dioceses require appropriate structures to enable the mission and ministry of the Church to be exercised as effectively and efficiently as possible within their geographical area. All dioceses need boards and committees which can ensure that issues such as finance, pastoral reorganisation and education are fully considered. However, we believe that a degree of flexibility is necessary to allow dioceses to develop a board structure which they feel is appropriate. There are considerable variations between the dioceses, for example in size and sociological and demographic composition, and we favour over time some relaxation of the statutory framework which governs diocesan administration.

> '10.11 We commend to dioceses the spirit of our recommendations about the national level, especially where we recommend that the size of many boards should be reduced, that staff should be given greater executive authority (and be held accountable for it) and that a greater reliance should be placed on *ad hoc* working groups comprising members selected for their expertise. We encourage dioceses to adopt a constructive approach to any such changes at the national level and to consider how they might apply these principles to their own structures. We hope they and the Council will share in the dissemination of good practice. Dioceses must be rigorous in ensuring that their structures and their administration are, and remain, as effective and efficient as possible. There is considerable scope within the existing legislation to make changes – and we are aware that some dioceses are already taking advantage of this – and we hope that a partnership with the national level will

develop which will facilitate the passage of legislation to allow greater flexibility in certain areas currently regulated by statute.'

We fully endorse those views, and make some suggestions in the following paragraphs for achieving flexibility.

(A) THE DBF

6.25   In paragraph 6.15 above we referred to the fact that a number of dioceses have considered it appropriate and helpful to seek to bring together considerations of policy and the allocation of resources by examining the structural relationship between the DBF and the diocesan synod/bishop's council. We take the view that it should be for each diocese to make such arrangements in this area as will best suit its particular circumstances, although we have already recommended that there should be an amendment to the statutory functions of the diocesan synod to provide that it should receive the annual accounts and approve the budget for the diocese (paragraphs 6.5 and 6.6 above).

6.26   We have been made aware, however, that there are legislative complications in making provision for there to be common membership as between the DBF and the diocesan synod. These arise from the provisions of the Diocesan Boards of Finance Measure 1925 (the 1925 Measure), which was on the statute book before the inception of the 1969 Measure, and which many consider to be outdated in a number of respects.

6.27   Under the provisions of the 1925 Measure, as amended, every diocesan synod must constitute a DBF which is to be registered under the Companies Act with powers to hold property, to transact business on behalf of the diocese and to act as a committee of the diocesan synod. The membership of the company must include the diocesan bishop and such other members drawn from the diocesan synod and elsewhere as the articles prescribe but with the overriding proviso that the majority shall be laity.

6.28   Sixteen dioceses have already changed their DBF memorandum and articles in order to make the DBF membership the same as that of the diocesan synod. We understand they have been advised that this is permissible under the terms of existing legislation. It appears to us, however, to be at least open to doubt whether the requirement of the Church Representation Rules that 'the numbers of the houses of clergy and laity are [to be] approximately equal' (Rule 31 (8)) can be reconciled with the provision in the 1925 Measure that a majority of the DBF are to be laity.

6.29   If it is desired to bring the policy-making responsibility of the synod and the financial responsibilities of the DBF closer together, there are two models, one with two sub-models, to be examined. First, there is the model in which the functions of the DBF and the diocesan synod are performed by the same body. In this model a separate financial executive would be needed which would be subordinate to the synod. Secondly, it might be appropriate to have the DBF as a body separate from the synod, either with separate membership or with the same membership as the bishop's council. We do not think it is sensible to have the members of the bishop's council acting as the financial executive because many of the council's members are likely to have been elected for qualities other than their financial expertise. If therefore the council doubles as the DBF, a subordinate financial executive will be needed. If, however, the DBF has a separate membership, it is reasonable to expect it to have the skills necessary to manage the diocese's finances without the need for a separate executive. A common element in all these models would be provision for the submission of a draft budget to the synod through the bishop's council by whichever body was, in effect, the financial executive.

6.30   In view of the fact that each diocese must have a corporate body for the purpose of (*inter alia*) issuing contracts to employees and holding property, it will be easier for the DBF to remain in being than to abolish it. But in all models **where the DBF and the diocesan synod are not identical we recommend that the DBF should be subordinate to the resolutions of the diocesan synod. We also recommend that the 1925 Measure be amended or replaced to remove existing doubts about the legality of establishing a single body to perform the functions of both the diocesan synod and the DBF and otherwise so as to provide flexibility for dioceses to make arrangements for the conduct of their financial business which best suit their circumstances.**

(B)   DIOCESAN BOARDS AND COMMITTEES

6.31   In addition to the bishop's council and standing committee and the DBF, statute requires each diocese to establish:

(i)   a parsonages board (Repair of Benefice Buildings Measure 1972, section 1);

(ii)   a pastoral committee (Pastoral Measure 1983, section 1);

(iii)   a redundant churches uses committee (Pastoral Measure 1983, section 42 (1));

(iv)   a board of patronage (Patronage (Benefices) Measure 1986, section 26);

(v)   a diocesan advisory committee (Care of Churches and Ecclesiastical Jurisdiction Measure 1991, section 2);

(vi)   a diocesan board of education (Diocesan Boards of Education Measure 1991, section 1);

(vii)   a vacancy in see committee (Vacancy in See Committee Regulations 1993).

6.32   All these boards and committees have important statutory functions to perform. We have considered whether, in relation to any of those functions, we could recommend some 'relaxation of the statutory framework' of the kind suggested in paragraph 10.10 of the Turnbull Report which we have quoted above.

6.33   The Repair of Benefice Buildings Measure 1972 already allows the DBF to be designated as the board for the purposes of the Measure, i.e. to function as the parsonages board. Many dioceses have adopted this sensible course and we draw it to the attention of other dioceses who may have overlooked it.

6.34   The diocesan pastoral committee has important statutory duties under the Pastoral Measure 1983 (the 1983 Measure) in relation to initiating proposals which may mature into pastoral schemes and carrying out necessary consultations in connection therewith (see sections 2 and 3). The constitution and procedure of the committee are defined in detail by Schedule I to the Measure. In practice we are told that in many dioceses the pastoral work is done by sub-committees and the diocesan pastoral committee, as such, only meets once a year to discharge its statutory obligation to report annually to the diocesan synod. The committee has power under paragraph 10 of Schedule I to appoint sub-committees, to appoint members of sub-committees who are not members of the main committee and to delegate to such sub-committees any of their functions under Part I and Part IV of the Measure with the exceptions mentioned in paragraph 10 of Schedule I. However, that paragraph stipulates that the majority of members of any such sub-committees shall be members of the main committee. The evidence before us suggested that the pastoral work of the dioceses could be done more effectively and economically if this restriction on the membership of sub-committees were removed. We are confident that diocesan pastoral committees can be relied upon to ensure that a sub-committee to whom any of their functions are to be delegated will have a suitably responsible membership. **We accordingly recommend that paragraph 10 of Schedule I to the 1983 Measure be amended so as to remove the requirement that the majority of members of a sub-committee appointed under that paragraph shall be members of the diocesan pastoral committee.**

6.35   The only duty of the diocesan redundant churches uses committee is '. . . to make every endeavour to find suitable alternative uses for redundant buildings in their dioceses.' In practice, the search for a suitable alternative use for a church which is likely to be or has been declared redundant is often undertaken by members of the diocesan staff or by an outside agency employed for the purpose and the committee's function is effectively limited to endorsing the suitability of suggested alternative uses where the search has been successful. The constitution of the committee is prescribed by paragraphs 5 to 12 of Schedule V to the 1983 Measure. The question has been raised before us whether it is really necessary to impose on a diocese the obligation to appoint and maintain a separately constituted committee to perform this very limited function, when, in most cases, the pastoral committee or one of its sub-committees will have been closely concerned with the circumstances leading to the redundancy. **We recommend that the 1983 Measure be amended to provide that, where the diocesan synod so resolves, the functions of the diocesan redundant churches uses committee under section 42 may be performed by the diocesan pastoral committee or by any sub-committee, thereof to whom any relevant function may be delegated under paragraph 10 of Schedule I of the 1983 Measure and that, so long as such a** resolution is in force, the proceedings of the redundant churches uses committee shall be suspended.

6.36   For the rest, we do not think that any significant gain in simplicity or flexibility is to be achieved by amendment of any of the other Measures referred to in paragraph 6.31. **We accordingly recommend no change.**

6.37   In addition to these statutory boards and committees, there are many which are non-statutory. We are aware that many dioceses are reviewing, or have recently reviewed, their board and committee structure, in some cases following the publication of the recommendations of the Turnbull Report about analogous arrangements at the national level. These are matters fully within the competence of dioceses to decide. We commend to them the need to keep the effectiveness of all boards and committees under review from time to time.

The office of diocesan secretary

6.38   We end this survey of issues raised with us about the diocesan level of synodical government with a brief look at the position of the diocesan secretary. This post is non-statutory and the fact that it is so has, in the past, posed difficulties where it would be more appropriate to refer in legislation to one administrative officer of the diocese rather than have to invent an office or give yet another task to the diocesan bishop or archdeacon when, *de facto*, the task will be carried out by the diocesan secretary.

6.39   There is a variety of functions which can only be carried out by a diocesan officer with a legal persona. **We recommend that statutory provision should be made which will give the diocesan secretary a legal persona and which will also allow dioceses themselves to allocate to their secretary such functions as they deem appropriate.**

6.40   Reference to the office of diocesan secretary provides us with an opportunity to pay tribute not only to the holders of that office but to their staff, to diocesan registrars, and to the many other holders of posts (paid and unpaid) who between them ensure the smooth functioning of synodical government and administration in the diocese. To them, and to the many who give freely of their time and talents to serve the Church as members of diocesan synods and committees, we wish to extend recognition and thanks.

7

The Convocations

7.1   Having considered synodical government in the parish, the deanery and the diocese, we come now to examine its operation at the provincial and national level. We begin by considering the oldest conciliar elements still surviving within our present arrangements – the Convocations of Canterbury and York.

7.2   The Convocations of the Provinces of Canterbury and York are the descendants of the ancient ecclesiastical councils of the Archbishops. Their functions have changed greatly over the centuries. The first assemblies which bore the name Convocations were constituted as representative of the clergy at all levels for the purpose of obtaining their consent to the taxation of the clergy. These bodies were gradually assimilated with the provincial synods of still earlier origin and assumed their function of legislating in ecclesiastical matters.

7.3   At the Reformation the Convocations' power to legislate by Canon became subject to control by the Crown, but it continued to be exercised until the early part of the eighteenth century. The Convocations then lapsed into a state of virtual suspension until their revival in the second half of the nineteenth century. In this century their resumed power to legislate by Canon continued to be exercised until it was transferred to the General Synod under the authority of the 1969 Measure. The members of the Upper and Lower Houses of the two Convocations now form the membership of the House of Bishops and the House of Clergy of the General Synod. But the Convocations as such still remain the representative assemblies of the clergy in the two Provinces. (The history briefly summarised here will be found more fully developed in the historical note which appears as Appendix I.)

7.4   The functions of the Convocations are now so attenuated that the question inevitably arises whether they continue to perform any role of sufficient importance and value in the life of the Church to justify their continued existence as distinct institutions within the formal structure of the Church's government. Of all the Church's institutions, the Convocations have attracted the least comment from those who have made representations to us. This in itself, no doubt, reflects the diminished role which they now play. Among those few who have commented, a number questioned the usefulness of the Convocations and at least one diocese regarded them as positively out of place in a rational system for the ordering of the Church's affairs.

7.5   On the other hand, those who favoured their retention were concerned for the maintenance of the separate identity of the Provinces, which they saw the continued existence of the two Convocations as protecting. They also urged that there is a valuable tradition of reflective debate in the Convocations on doctrinal matters which should not be lost, and that it is in the Convocations that some issues can most appropriately be canvassed by the clergy in the presence of their bishops. Consistent with this, on 21 February 1995 the Lower House of the Convocation of Canterbury, following a debate on the continuing role of Convocation, passed a motion to the effect 'That this House affirms the active continuation of Convocation in any future synodical revision of Church government.' The primary emphasis in the debate was on the role of Convocation as a focus for theological reflection and for consultation between bishops and clergy.

7.6   The only power of any significance in the formal government of the Church which is still exercisable by the Convocations as separate institutions is that which they enjoy by virtue of Article 7 of the Constitution of the General Synod in relation to any legislative 'provision touching doctrinal formulae or the services or ceremonies of the Church of England or the administration of the sacraments or sacred rites thereof.' (Article 7 is reproduced in full at Appendix III.10.) The effect of this enactment is that, if either House of either of the Convocations (or the House of Laity of the General Synod) so requires, any provision in the category defined by Article 7 (which for convenience we describe as 'the Article 7 category') must be referred to the Convocations (and to the House of Laity) and will be considered by each House of each of the Convocations (and by the House of Laity) sitting separately. If the provision is rejected by two or more of the four Houses of the Convocations or by the House of Laity, the same or a similar provision may not be proposed again until after the election of a new General Synod. But, if only one House of one Convocation has objected, the provision may be referred to the Convocations again and, if the one House only still maintains its objection, that objection can then be overridden on a third reference to the House of Bishops and the House of Clergy of the General Synod by a two-thirds majority vote in each House.

7.7   The position at the present time under Article 7 is to be contrasted with that which obtained for 50 years before the 1969 Measure came into force, when a legislative provision of a kind falling within the Article 7 category might be enacted either in a Canon made by the Convocations or in a Measure passed by the Church Assembly. The Constitution of the Church Assembly did make special provision for Measures in the Article 7 category in that any such Measure was to be 'debated and voted upon by each of the three Houses sitting separately' and, as under Article 7, any such Measure could only be finally approved in the terms proposed by the House of Bishops. Thus, before 1970, the position was that a legislative provision in the Article 7 category could be enacted by the Church Assembly independently of the Convocations or by the Convocations independently of the Church Assembly.

7.8   In the light of this, now that the power to legislate either by Canon or by Measure is vested in the General Synod, it is difficult to see any logic underlying the elaborate and extremely complex procedure prescribed by Article 7 for the sole purpose of giving to the Upper or Lower House of the Convocations in each Province a power to frustrate or to delay legislation which is acceptable to all three Houses of the General Synod. It seems likely that Article 7 was part of the compromise which underlay the recommendations of the Hodson Commission (to which reference is made in paragraph 18 of the historical note at Appendix I), which was designed to make the Convocations' loss of their power to legislate by Canon more acceptable.

7.9   Since the General Synod was established in 1970 Canons and Measures have from time to time been referred to the Convocations under Article 7 but on every such occasion the proposed legislation has been approved by both Houses of both Convocations, so that the delaying mechanism which is the *raison d'être* of the Article 7 procedure has never been put into operation. Taken together with the considerations to which we have drawn attention in the foregoing paragraph this leads us to the unhesitating conclusion that the function reserved to the Convocations under Article 7 no longer serves any necessary or useful purpose and should be discontinued. **We accordingly recommend that the provisions of Article 7 (2) to (6) of the Constitution of the General Synod be repealed and replaced by a simple requirement, similar to that formerly contained in the Constitution of the Church Assembly, that any provision falling within the Article 7 category shall be debated and voted upon by each of the three Houses of the General Synod sitting separately.**

7.10   The only other legislative power exercisable by the Convocations is that reserved to them by Canon H1 to make provision where necessary by instrument in relation to their own Provinces. No significant use of this power has been made since the General Synod came into being and here again we cannot see that any necessary or useful purpose would be served by its retention. If it were at any time desirable to legislate for one Province of the Church of England alone (and we find it difficult to conceive of the circumstances in which it would be), this could be done through the General Synod.

7.11   If, therefore, as we think, the Convocations should have no continuing powers to exercise in the General Synod's legislative process or in legislating separately for their own Provinces, they can only continue, if at all, as deliberative and consultative bodies. We do not doubt the value which, in the past, their deliberations have from time to time contributed to the Church's thinking. But we do not see how this function alone can justify their continued existence as formal bodies within the Church of England's governing structure, with the expenditure of time, energy and money in the continuance of their meetings and formal procedures and rules which this involves.

7.12   If the Archbishop of either Province wishes in future to consult the representative clergy of his Province or to invite their collective view on some theological issue or other significant matter of concern which has arisen, we see no obstacle to his calling an *ad hoc* meeting of the bishops and clergy of his Province who are also members of the General Synod without the need for specific statutory authority to do so. If there is a strong feeling among the clergy that there should be in place some machinery whereby a given number of them may be empowered to require the calling of such a meeting to debate a specific issue of concern to them, we think it would be appropriate to make provision by Measure to that effect. In either or both of these ways we believe that, by ensuring that the valued deliberative and consultative functions presently exercised by the Convocations are called into play only when required, these functions can be more effectively and economically preserved than by the continuance of the Convocations.

7.13   The report of the Lowe Commission in 1958[1] recommended that the fuller participation of the laity in the government of the Church of England, which was then generally accepted as a desirable objective, should be attained by the creation of a new House of Laity in each of the Convocations. If this had been implemented, the Convocations might well have developed a significant governmental role. But the ensuing debates led to a different conclusion and to the centralisation of Church government in the General Synod (see paragraph 18 of the historical note at Appendix I). We think it only realistic to recognise that the Convocations have since become something of an historical anachronism.

7.14   **We therefore recommend that the Convocations should cease to exist; and that, in consequence, the suffragan bishops elected to the House of Bishops and the members of the House of Clergy of the General Synod should be directly elected on the same basis, subject to the changes recommended in Chapter 8, as that which presently governs elections to the Convocations.**

7.15   At present the Lower House of each Convocation elects its own Prolocutor and Standing Committee. The two Prolocutors then become joint Chairmen of the House of Clergy of the General Synod. Under the House's Standing Orders the Prolocutors carry out the functions of Chairman in alternate years. If our recommendations in the foregoing paragraph are implemented, it will be for the House of

---

1   *The Convocations and the Laity*, C.A. 1240, Church Information Board, 1958.

Clergy to make provision in its Standing Orders, as the House of Laity does at present, for the election of its officers. The House will thus be able to consider whether it wishes, for example, to secure a balance of provincial representation amongst its officers or to impose any other restrictions on their election.

8

The General Synod

(1) Functions and composition

The General Synod

8.1   It is not perhaps surprising that, in the evidence we received, the General Synod attracted a good deal of criticism. It is a large body (575 members) with a high public profile which occasionally has to tackle big issues about which people hold widely different views with great conviction. Many church people who are affected by the decisions the General Synod makes know little about its workings, and may not know any of those who represent them on it. This combination of factors makes the General Synod an easy target for criticism, and the submissions to us bore this out.

8.2   The main criticisms of the General Synod made in evidence were that:

- it is too large;

- it tries to cover too wide an agenda;

- it is too much of a talking shop;

- it is too expensive and bureaucratic;

- it is not representative;

- its work should be set more fully within a context of prayer and worship;

- its procedures are too parliamentary and cumbersome;

- it meets too often;

- poor communication has led to a gulf between the General Synod and the parishes;

- the House of Bishops has, to some people, too much power, and to others, not enough.

8.3   These criticisms raise theological issues (which we discussed in Chapter 2), issues relating to the style and procedures of the Synod (which we address in Chapter 9) and to the electoral base (which we discuss in Chapter 10), and the question of communications between each level of synodical government (which we consider in Chapter 12). In this chapter we consider the functions, composition and size of the General Synod.

The functions of the General Synod

8.4   The functions of the General Synod are prescribed by paragraph 6 of Schedule 2 to the 1969 Measure (this is reproduced in full at Appendix III.11). The primary statutory function of the General Synod is 'to consider matters concerning the Church of England and to make provision in respect thereof' by Measure, Canon or regulation. The second function of the Synod, set out in paragraph 6 (b) of Schedule 2 to the Measure, is 'to consider and express their opinion on any other matters of religious or public interest.'

8.5   The first focuses on the Synod's primary role as a subordinate legislature, the second on its role in articulating a representative Church view on current issues. Although some might argue that the latter provision is cast in such wide terms as to invite the Synod to offer a view on virtually everything, any attempt to circumscribe the scope of the provision would, in our view, be likely to raise more difficulties than it settled. It is not the statutory scope of Synod's functions which is the issue but how it chooses to exercise them on any particular occasion. (We touch on some aspects of this in Chapter 9.) **We therefore recommend no amendment to the Synod's present statutory functions.**

Membership of the General Synod

8.6   The membership of the General Synod presently comprises three Houses:

(i)   The Upper Houses of the Convocations of Canterbury and York come together to form the House of Bishops. Under Canon H3 each of the Upper Houses comprises the diocesan

57

bishops of the Province together with such persons elected 'by and from among the suffragan bishops of the Province and other persons in episcopal orders working in a diocese of the Province who are members of the House of Bishops of that diocese' (six for Canterbury and three for York).

(ii) The Lower Houses of the two Convocations come together to form the House of Clergy of the General Synod. Canon H2 (see Appendix III.12) sets out the detailed provisions as to the membership of each of the Lower Houses.

(iii) The House of Laity is elected by the lay members of deanery synods and its membership is prescribed by the provisions made by Rules 35 and 42 of the Church Representation Rules (see Appendix III.13).

(iv) Appendix III.14 sets out the total membership, analysed according to its various sub-groups, of the present General Synod.

8.7   We have already recommended that the Upper and Lower Houses of the Convocations of Canterbury and York should cease to exist (paragraph 7.14 above) and also that the statutory requirement for deanery synods to be part of the formal structure of synodical government should be repealed (paragraph 5.19 above). Those two recommendations will require, if they are adopted, amendments to the present provisions of Canon Law and of the Church Representation Rules.

8.8   There are also, however, a number of other provisions, both in the Canons and the rules, which, we believe, merit further examination. These concern the provisions made for the representation of 'special constituencies' in the General Synod. It is to these that we now turn.

'Special constituencies'

8.9   Provision is made under Canons H2 and H3 and by the Church Representation Rules for representation of 'special constituencies' within each of the three Houses of the General Synod. We have examined the case for the continuation of each of these 'special constituencies.' In doing so our guiding principle has been to consider whether, in relation to membership of the House of Clergy and the House of Laity in particular, the membership of the respective Houses should be left as one for decision by the electorate of each House as a whole, or whether the case for the continuation of some special arrangement is still made out. Our general approach has been to consider whether those who are presently elected by 'special constituencies' have, or should be provided with, the opportunity to stand as candidates, and to vote, in the same way as other clergy and lay people in dioceses. Our view is that, save in quite exceptional cases, such provision should be the means through which they are represented on the General Synod.

The House of Bishops

(A)   DIOCESAN BISHOPS

8.10   All diocesan bishops are ex-officio members of the House of Bishops and therefore of the General Synod. We believe it is right, and indeed essential, that all diocesan bishops should continue to be ex-officio members of that House and of the General Synod. There is, nevertheless, a question whether, in the event of his unavoidable absence, provision should be made for a diocesan bishop, perhaps with the consent of the Archbishop of the Province, to nominate one of his suffragan bishops to represent him in the proceedings of the General Synod. The argument for this would be the desirability of ensuring that at all times the episcopal leadership of a diocese is present to contribute to, and draw from, discussion of issues in the General Synod. The argument against would be that it would open the way to the fielding of substitutes and might discourage diocesan bishops from attending the Synod; it is also the case that in five dioceses (Bradford, Leicester, Portsmouth, Newcastle and Sodor and Man) there is no suffragan bishop. If, nevertheless, such an arrangement were thought appropriate it could mirror the provisions which the House of Bishops has already incorporated into its own Standing Orders. These provide that, in carefully defined circumstances (illness, sabbatical leave, or duty in the House of Lords) and not therefore as a matter of generality, a diocesan bishop may recommend to the Archbishop of the Province the name of a suffragan bishop to attend the meeting of the House, with the right to speak but not to vote. (No such recommendation may however be made if a suffragan bishop from the diocese is already an elected member of the House.) This is not, we believe, a matter for us but rather one which the House of Bishops itself should consider and, if it thinks it appropriate, bring forward a proposal.

(B) SUFFRAGAN BISHOPS

8.11   At present nine suffragan bishops are elected from amongst the total number of suffragans as members of the Upper Houses of the Convocations (see paragraph 8.6 (i) above) and therefore to the House of Bishops. We believe it is right that suffragan bishops should continue to be eligible to stand for election to membership of the House. However, in line with our general view that, wherever possible, the size of the General Synod should be reduced, **we recommend that the provisions of Canon H3 and the rules made thereunder which provide for the election of six suffragan bishops to the Upper House of the Convocation of Canterbury, and three to the Upper House of the Convocation of York, be replaced by a provision that four shall be elected by their peers to the House of Bishops from the Province of Canterbury and two shall be so elected from the Province of York.**

(C) THE BISHOP OF DOVER

8.12   We received from the Archbishop of Canterbury a suggestion that the Bishop of Dover should be an ex-officio member of the House of Bishops, with the right not only to be present at its meetings and to speak (which he does under the House's Standing Orders) but also to vote in its proceedings. This would carry with it full ex-officio membership of the General Synod. In circumstances under which, for wholly understandable and proper reasons, the Archbishop delegates to the Bishop of Dover the great majority of the episcopal responsibilities for the diocese of Canterbury, we have concluded that this is a suggestion which we should commend. We do so recognising the unique wider responsibilities which the Archbishop of Canterbury has in relation to the Anglican Communion. **We therefore recommend that the Bishop of Dover be an ex-officio member of the House of Bishops and the General Synod and that Canon H3 be amended accordingly.**

(D) PROVINCIAL EPISCOPAL VISITORS (PEVS)

8.13   We have considered whether special representation within the House should be provided for PEVs. These offices were created by the Episcopal Ministry Act of Synod 1993 in order to facilitate the provision of extended episcopal oversight to those who are opposed to the ordination of women to the priesthood.

8.14   The three PEVs exercise episcopal ministry across diocesan boundaries with the permission of the diocesan bishop. A PCC may resolve to seek extended episcopal oversight and the diocesan bishop decides how this is to be provided. In some dioceses this will be through a suffragan, area, assistant or retired bishop but others will make use of the PEV. PEVs also provide episcopal care and support to individual clergy or laity who are opposed to the ordination of women to the priesthood.

8.15   For synodical purposes PEVs are treated in the same way as other suffragan bishops; they may stand for election and vote as suffragans within their respective Provinces. In addition to membership of the diocesan synod of the diocese to which he is suffragan a PEV may also be invited to be a member of the diocesan synod in the diocese where he resides (Rule 30 (7) (b) of the Church Representation Rules). The House of Bishops has amended its own standing orders to provide that all three PEVs, if not elected to the House, nevertheless have the right to attend and address all meetings of the House but without the right to vote in its proceedings.

8.16   We have received representations that PEVs should be more directly represented on the General Synod. Some have argued that all PEVs should be ex-officio members, others that the PEVs should elect one of their number to represent them, and other variations have also been put forward.

8.17   In recognition that there exist within the Church of England both those who are in favour of and those who are opposed to the ordination of women to the priesthood (both views being held with equal integrity), we are unanimous in believing that the views of both must be heard in the General Synod. However we are not agreed as to how this is best achieved.

8.18   Those who support a special constituency for PEVs argue that this would guarantee the presence in the House of at least one opponent of the ordination of women to the priesthood. Because this view is in the minority, they argue, such representation cannot be guaranteed by relying on the present voting system to produce at least one opponent bishop from among the suffragans. There is no guarantee that in the future any diocesan bishops would be opponents of women's ordination even though at present that position is represented among diocesans. A new constituency, however small, would be a sign that the Church recognises and respects the position of PEVs and those whom they represent.

8.19   On the other hand there are those who argue that if the Church is genuinely committed to a position of equal respect for both views it must ensure that they are both represented amongst the diocesan bishops, who are ex-officio members of the General Synod. They are so represented at present. It might even be argued that creating a special constituency would in effect reduce the need to have diocesan bishops from both integrities and thus weaken rather than strengthen the representation in the Synod of the present minority position.

8.20   In coming to a decision on this matter the Synod will need to bear in mind that, on the one hand:

- the Act of Synod was passed by the General Synod 'to make provision for the continuing diversity of opinion in the Church of England as to the ordination and ministry of women as priests;'

- this is a highly sensitive issue on which the decision could result in the opponents of the ordination of women to the priesthood feeling increasingly marginalised in the Church.

On the other hand:

- there is no precedent for reserving seats in the General Synod for those who hold a particular view on one specific issue;

- the thrust of many of the representations made to us has been to reduce the number of special constituencies rather than create more.

8.21   In the light of the reductions we are recommending in the special constituencies we are all agreed that, if it were decided by the Synod to establish a special constituency for PEVs, they should elect only one from among their number, and that the creation of a special constituency should mean that PEVs would be excluded from taking part in the election of other suffragan bishops to the House of Bishops. **However, by a majority we do not recommend the creation of a special constituency for PEVs.**

The House of Clergy

(A)   DEANS AND PROVOSTS

8.22   Under the provisions of Canon H2 (Appendix III.12 paragraph 1(a)) ten deans and provosts are elected to the House from the Province of Canterbury and five from the Province of York.

8.23   The report of the Archbishops' Commission on Cathedrals[1] recommended, *inter alia*, that 'all cathedrals should be given a recognised place in the structure of synodical government' (Chapter 6, paragraph 27) and that there should be established a roll made up of those 'recognised as regular or habitual worshippers or who are otherwise regularly involved in the work of the cathedral.' (Chapter 6, paragraph 24)

8.24 ·   Draft legislation to implement the range of recommendations made in that report is presently before the Synod. The question for us has been whether the present provisions of Canon H2 which reserve 15 places on the General Synod for deans and provosts remain appropriate for the purposes of securing for cathedrals a 'recognised place in the structure of synodical government.'

8.25   Cathedrals are increasingly working together as a cohesive body through the Deans and Provosts Conference and the Association of English Cathedrals. Such factors as the advent of state aid for the upkeep of cathedral fabric and the implementation of the recommendations of the Archbishops' Commission have encouraged this development. The contribution of the 15 elected deans and provosts to the General Synod is considerable.

---

1   *Heritage and Renewal,* Church House Publishing, 1994.

8.26   Notwithstanding this and the significant role which cathedrals have in the local and regional life and work of the Church, and some in its national life, cathedrals are a component part of the diocese. Many cathedrals have sought to strengthen their role as the 'mother church' of the diocese. Whilst they all have, in differing degrees, a distinctive role, so too do other institutions (for instance theological colleges) for whom no special provision is made. Cathedrals also have the opportunity to be represented in other ways – through residentiary canons and lay people who can, and do, stand for election to the General Synod. The fact that a number of residentiary canons are elected to the House of Clergy encourages us to be confident that cathedrals would continue to be well represented in the General Synod if the present provisions concerning deans and provosts were not in place.

8.27   We believe it should be for the clergy of the diocese to decide whether or not to elect their dean or provost as a member of the House of Clergy. **We therefore recommend that the provisions of Canon H2 and the rules made thereunder which secure 15 places in the House of Clergy of the General Synod for deans and provosts elected by their peers be repealed and that deans and provosts should be qualified as electors and eligible for election to the House of Clergy of the General Synod from their dioceses.**

(B)   THE COLLEGIATE CHURCHES OF ST PETER IN WESTMINSTER AND OF ST GEORGE WINDSOR AND THE CATHEDRAL CHURCH OF THE HOLY TRINITY IN GIBRALTAR

8.28   Canon H2 1 (a) includes the deans of these three churches among those who may presently be elected by and from among the deans and provosts to the Lower House of the Convocation of Canterbury. In the light of our recommendation in the previous paragraph we also **recommend that the deans and the residentiary canons of those churches should be qualified as electors and be eligible for election to the House of Clergy of the General Synod within the dioceses of London, Oxford and Gibraltar in Europe respectively.**

(C)   THE DEAN OF JERSEY AND THE DEAN OF GUERNSEY

8.29   The rules made under Canon H2, paragraph 1 (b), provide that the Dean of Jersey and the Dean of Guernsey shall serve alternately as members of the Lower House of the Convocation of Canterbury (and therefore of the General Synod). We do not believe it is appropriate to reserve a place on the Synod for the deans of the Channel Islands. All beneficed and licensed clergy in the two deaneries (including these two deans) should be eligible to stand for election as representatives of the diocese of Winchester and to vote in those elections (see also paragraph 8.48 below). **We recommend therefore that the provisions in Canon H2, paragraph 1(b) should be repealed.**

(D)   ARCHDEACONS

8.30   The presence of archdeacons in the two Convocations dates from the beginning of these institutions. The Convocations were essentially parliamentary bodies and their purpose was to obtain consent to royal taxation of the clergy; thus those who could contribute most, the bishops and rich foundations, were given greater representation than the parochial clergy. The role of the archdeacons was mainly administrative. As legal officers, with courts and officials, they issued the citations, conducted the proctorial elections, collected the taxes when they had been voted, and pursued defaulters. The ancient Convocations thus had strong ex-officio majorities, even after the Reformation, with the deans and archdeacons forming a major part of the two Lower Houses.

8.31   It remains the case that archdeacons of the Church of England have a role which is distinct from that of the bishop or parish priest. As *Oculus Episcopi* (the eye of the bishop) an archdeacon will be involved with legal and practical matters concerning visitations, clergy care, discipline matters, faculties and quinquennial inspections. Much work in these, and other, areas is directly affected by the legislation which the General Synod approves. It is therefore appropriate that archdeacons should have the opportunity to be represented on the General Synod.

8.32   At present, under Canon H2 paragraph 1 (c), one archdeacon from every diocese is automatically a member of the House of Clergy. If not chosen as the representative archdeacon for the diocese, archdeacons are also free, however, to stand for election by the clergy of their dioceses and a number do. We do not believe it right that archdeacons should have these two separate routes for election to the

Synod. As in the case of all 'special constituencies', we have considered whether there should be any prescribed provision which would automatically secure for 43 archdeacons membership of the General Synod. We have concluded that, in the circumstances of synodical life in the late twentieth century, it should properly be a matter for the electors in the diocese to determine who should represent them.

8.33   Archdeacons, we believe, should be eligible to stand for election in the same way as other clergy. A number do so, successfully, at present. As with deans and provosts, we are confident that a sufficient number will be elected by this route to Synod to ensure that their valuable contribution continues to be heard. **We therefore recommend that the provisions of Canon H2 and the rules made thereunder which secure a place for an archdeacon chosen by his peers in each diocese be repealed.**

(E)   SERVICE CHAPLAINS

8.34   Paragraph 1 (d) of Canon H2 provides for ex-officio membership of the General Synod for the Chaplain of the Fleet, the Chaplain-General of the Forces and the Chaplain-in-Chief, Royal Air Force.

8.35   We received in evidence from the Forces Synodical Council[2] a request for enhanced membership of the General Synod. They were concerned that, although the forces had ex-officio representation in the House of Clergy, they were unrepresented in both the House of Bishops and in the House of Laity and that the chaplains were prevented from standing for election to the House of Clergy. They argued a case for making the Bishop to the Forces an ex-officio member of the House of Bishops and for increasing their representation in the House of Clergy by six – each service to elect two chaplains. They also sought amendments to the Church Representation Rules to provide that the services should have a minimum of six lay people elected to the House of Laity.

---

2   In January 1989, the Archbishop of Canterbury, as the bishop responsible for Her Majesty's armed forces, confirmed (with the concurrence of the relevant boards at the Ministry of Defence) rules for synodical representation in the armed forces. These provide that each service should establish an electoral roll, each should elect houses of clergy and laity to an archdeaconry synod for each of those services and that the synods should form the Forces Synodical Council.

8.36   We recognise that clergy and laity in the services are in a special position in relation to elections to the General Synod in that they are not necessarily in a position to stand for election or to vote in the usual way under Canon H2 or under the Church Representation Rules. In this sense they are in something of a unique position. We are therefore persuaded that, on the grounds of equity and of proper access to the national councils of the Church, some special provision is required, although not to the extent requested.

8.37   We do not, however, believe it would be appropriate to provide for ex-officio membership of the Bishop to the Forces in the House of Bishops. The Archbishop of Canterbury is the episcopal ordinary to the armed forces and we believe that he is in a position sufficiently to represent their interests and reflect their concerns to the House.

8.38   Nor are we persuaded that representation from the forces in the House of Clergy should be increased from three to nine. We are persuaded that there should continue to be specific provision for representation from the three services in the House of Clergy. We do not believe, however, that it should be prescribed that the representation of the forces in the House should necessarily be through the ex-officio membership of each of the senior chaplains. **Instead we recommend that the provisions of Canon H2 which secure ex-officio places in the House of Clergy for the three senior chaplains of the armed forces should be replaced by a provision that the house of clergy of each of the three archdeaconry synods of the armed forces should elect one of their chaplains to the House of Clergy of the General Synod.** (We make a similar recommendation concerning representation from the forces in the House of Laity in paragraph 8.49 below.)

(F)   CHAPLAIN-GENERAL OF PRISONS

8.39   Under the provisions of Canon H2 paragraph 1 (d) the Chaplain-General of Prisons is also presently a member ex-officio of the General Synod. In this case as in others we have considered whether those concerned should, if they wished, stand for election in the usual way.

8.40   All prison chaplains are licensed by the bishop and are, therefore, free to stand for election to the House of Clergy of the General Synod from their dioceses. In this respect prison chaplains are in the same position as hospital chaplains and school chaplains, although through this provision of Canon H2 1 (d) they are treated differently in that the Chaplain-General has ex-officio representation on the General Synod. **We recommend that this provision be replaced by a provision that chaplains (including the Chaplain-General) should be eligible to stand for election to the House of Clergy of the General Synod from their dioceses.**

(G)   PROCTORS OF THE CLERGY

8.41   Canon H2 makes provision for the election to the Lower Houses of the Convocations of 'proctors of the clergy.' We have recommended in Chapter 7 that the Convocations should cease to exist and that the House of Clergy of the General Synod should be directly elected on the same basis as that which presently governs elections to the Convocations (see paragraph 7.14 above). Subject to that and to the recommendation we make later in this chapter about the number of clergy to be elected by each diocese, we recommend no change.

(H)   REPRESENTATIVES OF RELIGIOUS COMMUNITIES

8.42   Canon H2 1 (f) provides that one person chosen by and from among the religious communities in the Province of Canterbury in such manner as may be prescribed by rules made under the Canon shall be a member of the General Synod. The same provision is made in paragraph 1 (d) in respect of the Province of York. Under Rule 16 of the Clergy Representation Rules the electors 'shall be priests or deacons of the Church of England who are certified by the head of the religious community to be members of that community and are resident either in the Province of Canterbury or in the Province of York.'

8.43   In 1995 the House of Bishops agreed, on advice from the Advisory Council on the Relations of Bishops and Religious Communities, to differentiate between three distinct categories of religious community:

(i)   religious communities officially recognised by the House of Bishops as being within the received tradition of the Church, living under vows of stability, poverty, chastity and obedience and having representation on the General Synod and on the Advisory Council;

(ii)   religious communities acknowledged by the House to be living a corporate Christian life within the Anglican Church, to whom the Advisory Council may give advice and assistance, if requested; and

(iii)   other Christian communities, groups and networks associated with the National Association of Christian Communities and Networks.

Only those communities in category (i) above are officially recognised communities and it is only the members of those who are entitled to be candidates and to vote, in elections to the General Synod. As we have explained in paragraph 8.9 above, in our view it should only be in quite exceptional cases that provision should be made for members of the General Synod to be elected through special arrangements. We are persuaded, however, that it would not be practicable to recommend that members of religious communities should be required to stand and vote in those elections alongside other clergy (or indeed laity – see paragraph 8.47 below) in dioceses. The nature of each of the communities concerned varies enormously – some are concentrated in one location, in others the members are widely dispersed. In this respect, if in no other, an analogy may be drawn with members of the armed forces. It would not be reasonable, in our view, to expect that they could secure election unless some special provision for them is continued. **We therefore recommend that the communities should continue to be eligible to elect representatives, both clerical and lay, to the General Synod. We take the view however that the number of clerical representatives should be reduced from two to one and, accordingly, also recommend that the provisions of Canon H2 and of the rules made thereunder (see paragraph 8.42 above) should be amended to provide that the clerical representative should be elected by the same electors as at present but that the election should no longer be held on a provincial basis. In paragraph 8.47 below we make our recommendations concerning the representation of lay members of religious communities.**

(I)   UNIVERSITY REPRESENTATIVES

8.44   Paragraph 3 of Canon H2 makes provision for the election of clerical representatives from the universities in each Province to the General Synod (four from the Province of Canterbury and two from the Province of York). Rule 12 of the Clergy Representation Rules (see Appendix III.15) makes provision as to who the electors shall be.

8.45   There is no provision made in the Canon, or in the Rules made under it, that those elected should have any particular theological expertise. In practice, however, it has been that kind of expertise that those elected have been able to bring to the General Synod and it has been much valued. We do not doubt that the General Synod is, and should continue to be, assisted in its deliberations by those with particular theological expertise. We are not persuaded however that this is necessarily available only through universities. For instance the staff of theological colleges and of Church colleges of further education (for whom no specific membership provisions are made) also have expertise to offer and a number of principals of theological colleges have been elected as proctors for their diocese. The present electoral base for this constituency is also very anomalous. The number of electors is small, ranging from four electors in the smallest constituency to thirty electors in the largest constituency. Eligibility to be an elector or to be a candidate is confined to clerks in Holy Orders and this causes resentment among those laity who are theologians at a university and members of the Church of England. Government policy of designating polytechnics as universities has greatly increased the number of universities which has added to the administrative burden of running such elections.

8.46   Consistent with our earlier conclusions, therefore, we do not believe it appropriate to retain specific provision for there to be representatives of universities in the House of Clergy. We believe that those concerned should stand as candidates in their dioceses. **We therefore recommend that paragraph 3 of Canon H2 should be repealed.**

The House of Laity

(A)   REPRESENTATIVES OF RELIGIOUS COMMUNITIES

8.47   Under Rule 35 (1) (b) of the Church Representation Rules three lay members of religious communities, two from the Province of Canterbury and one from the Province of York, are chosen by the lay members of religious communities to be members of the House of Laity of the General Synod (see Appendix III.13). As in the case of clerical members of such communities (see paragraph 8.43 above) we believe it right to continue special provisions for the representation of lay religious. **We recommend however that the number of lay representatives should be reduced from three to two, one each to be elected as at present by and from the communities in each Province.**

(B)   REPRESENTATIVES OF THE CHANNEL ISLANDS

8.48   In paragraph 8.29 above we discuss the present provisions for the Dean of Jersey or the Dean of Guernsey to be an ex-officio member of the General Synod. Under Rule 36 (1) of the Church Representation Rules two representatives of both deaneries are elected to the House of Laity of the General Synod in accordance with the provisions of the Channel Islands (Representation) Measure 1931. **We recommend that the Channel Islands (Representation) Measure 1931 be repealed and that, so far as necessary, Rule 36 of the Church Representation Rules be amended to provide that candidates from the deaneries of Jersey and Guernsey shall be eligible for election to the House of Laity in the same way as any other lay candidates from the diocese of Winchester.**

(C)   THE FORCES

8.49   In paragraph 8.35 above we set out the representations we received from the Forces Synodical Council. **For the same reasons as those set out in paragraph 8.38 above, we also recommend that the house of laity of each of the three archdeaconry synods should be entitled to elect one lay person to the House of Laity of the General Synod.**

Other membership issues

(A)   EX-OFFICIO MEMBERSHIP

8.50   At present the holders of the offices of the Dean of the Arches and Auditor, the Vicar General of each Province, the Third Church Estates Commissioner, and the chairman of the Church of England Pensions Board, who may be lay persons or in Holy Orders, are ex-officio members of the General Synod pursuant to the provisions of Canon H2 1 (g) (Canterbury) and (e) (York) or of Rule 42 (1) of the Church Representation Rules. The latter rule also provides that the

First and Second Church Estates Commissioners and the chairman of the Central Board of Finance shall be ex-officio members of the House of Laity. **We propose no change in these provisions because of the importance of the office each holds.** However, we note that draft legislation is presently before the Synod (the draft National Institutions Measure – GS 1228) which, if implemented in its present form, will affect the membership of the Church Commissioners and of the Central Board of Finance and the ex-officio membership of the Synod.

(B)   RETIRED CLERGY AND AN AGE LIMIT FOR LAY MEMBERS

8.51   At present clergy are required to retire at the age of 70 and many do so earlier. Once they have retired, unless they have a licence from their bishop, they cease to be eligible to stand as candidates in elections to the House of Clergy of the General Synod and they have no vote in those elections. Lay members of the General Synod are, on the other hand, wholly free to stand beyond that age as candidates for election to the House of Laity of the General Synod and, provided they are members of the House of Laity of their deanery synod, are entitled to vote in those elections.

8.52   It was represented to us that there was an anomaly here which might be resolved either by making it possible for retired clergy with a bishop's permission to officiate to be elected to the diocesan synod and to the General Synod, or by seeking to impose a maximum age limit above which lay people would cease to be eligible for election.

8.53   In Chapter 10 we make recommendations on both these issues (paragraphs 10.3 and 10.19 below).

(C)   REPRESENTATIVES OF OTHER CHURCHES

8.54   The Standing Orders of the General Synod (SO 113) provide that other Churches may be invited by the Standing Committee of the General Synod to send representatives to attend a group of sessions of the General Synod. These representatives have the right to speak in most debates but have no right to vote. The Standing Committee has invited seven Churches to send a representative each of whom serves for a period of three years. We very much welcome this provision in the Standing Orders and the wider perspective which ecumenical representatives have already brought to the Synod's deliberations. **We do not wish to propose any amendment of this Standing Order which is broadly consistent with the practice of a number of other Churches in inviting the Standing Committee to nominate members of the General Synod to attend their assemblies.**

(D)   ELIGIBILITY OF DIOCESAN STAFF TO SEEK ELECTION

8.55   Under Rule 37 (2):

'A person shall be disqualified from being nominated for election as a member of the General Synod if he holds any paid office or employment appointment [*sic*] which is or may be made or confirmed by the General Synod, the Convocations, the Central Board of Finance, the Church Commissioners for England (except that such disqualification shall not apply to any Commissioner so appointed in receipt of a salary or other emoluments), the Church of England Pensions Board or the Corporation of the Church House.'

8.56   The question was raised with us whether provision should also be made that persons holding any paid office or appointment with a DBF should be disqualified from eligibility to seek election as a member of the General Synod. Such a provision would clearly prevent all lay employees of a diocese (including diocesan secretaries) from standing for election. It would, however, also rule out ordained people including those holding part-time sector posts who had, under licence from the bishop, parochial responsibilities. We have concluded that it should remain a matter for the electorate to decide whether to vote for such persons in the elections to the General Synod.

The size of the Synod

8.57   Under Canon H3 the House of Bishops is made up of 53 members. Canon H2 2 (a) provides that the House of Clergy shall not exceed 250 elected members (not more than 170 for the Province of Canterbury and not more than 80 for the Province of York). Rule 36 (1) makes the same provision for the maximum number of elected representatives in the House of Laity. The General Synod determines the number of members to be elected to each House by each diocese, in the case of clergy in proportion to the number of clerical electors in the diocese and in the case of the House of Laity in proportion to the aggregate numbers on the electoral rolls of parishes in each diocese. Appendix III.14 sets out the present numbers of each House of the General Synod.

8.58   The present General Synod comprises 575 members in total. This number has remained almost constant since 1970. However, since 1970 there has been a reduction of 2,113 in the number of clerical electors (from 15,618 to 13,505 in 1995) and of 1,092,379 in the number of persons on electoral rolls of parishes (from 2,562,820 to 1,470,441 in 1995).

8.59   In the light of this reduction in the number of clerical and lay people represented by the Synod, we believe it appropriate that the size of the General Synod, and therefore of each of its constituent Houses, should be reduced. We are conscious that some may argue that this will weaken the Synod's representativeness but in view of the fall in numbers we have set out we do not agree. Moreover a smaller Synod will in our view encourage more effective representation by enabling a higher proportion of members to engage in discussion and by making interaction between representatives easier. It will also have benefits in terms of cost, demands on time, and ease of organisation. Concerns about the cost of the Synod (see paragraph 9.19 below), in terms of both money and time, were a constant theme in the evidence put to us.

8.60   We accordingly recommend that in future the size of the General Synod should be as shown as in the table below:

	Canterbury	York	Either Province	TOTAL
House of Bishops				
Diocesan Bishops	30	14		44
Elected Suffragan Bishops	4	2		6
The Bishop of Dover (ex-officio)	1			1
	35	16		51
House of Clergy				
Elected by dioceses	104	41		145
Elected by the House of Clergy of each of the Services' Archdeaconry Synods			3	3
Elected by Religious Communities			1	1
Co-opted places	3	2		5
	107	43	4	154
House of Laity				
Elected by dioceses	114	48		162
Elected by the House of Laity of each of the Services' Archdeaconry Synods			3	3
Elected by Religious Communities	1	1		2
Co-opted places			5	5
Ex officio (First and Second Church) Estates Commissioners and Chairman of CBF)			3	3
	115	49	11	175
Either House of Clergy or House of Laity				
Ex officio (Dean of Arches, the two Vicars General, the Third Church Estate Commissioner and the Chairman of the Pensions Board)			5	5
Appointed members			5	5
			10	10
TOTAL	257	108	25	390

Seven representatives of other Churches would continue to be appointed to the Synod under its Standing Orders with speaking but not voting rights.

8.61   This table does not take account of any additional ex-officio members for which provision may be made by the draft National Institutions Measure which is presently before the General Synod.

8.62   Under these arrangements each diocese (apart from Sodor and Man and Europe) would continue to elect at least three members to the House of Clergy and three members to the House of Laity. The number of members of the House of Clergy would be reduced from 259 to 154 and of the House of Laity from 258 to 175. The Schedule attached as Appendix III.16 sets out the number of representatives in each House which, under our proposals, would be elected by each diocese.

Representation of voluntary and mission societies

8.63   We have received requests that special representation should be provided in the General Synod for the voluntary societies (including the Children's Society and the Mothers' Union) who are members of the Anglican Voluntary Societies Forum and for those overseas mission agencies of the Church who are members of Partnership for World Mission. We have the highest regard for the work of these societies and we see the need to find mechanisms to ensure that partnership between the voluntary and official agencies of the Church is strengthened. We do not, however, think that the right way to achieve this is to provide a reserved place or places on the Synod for the voluntary bodies. As we have indicated earlier in this chapter we believe that membership of the General Synod should be determined primarily by the electorates in each diocese and that all candidates should put themselves forward, as they are already free to do, for election by that means. To create a new special constituency for the voluntary societies would be contrary to the thrust of our other recommendations.

Co-option and appointment

8.64   We recognise, however, that there is special expertise and experience from which the wider Church through the Synod would greatly benefit but which may not emerge through the electoral process. This is to some extent already recognised in the existing power of co-option of the Houses of Clergy and Laity, which, however, they have in practice exercised sparingly. **We recommend the retention of that power and that, in addition, the Archbishop of Canterbury and the Archbishop of York jointly should have power to appoint up to five people (clerical or lay) as members of the Synod so that such special expertise may, if it is thought desirable, be brought into the work of the Synod.**

9

The General Synod

(2) Style and procedures

9.1   Many of the matters we now discuss are of a kind about which it is impossible to legislate but which touch on the conduct of Synod and of its members. Although we set our observations in the context of the General Synod, a good deal of what we say is, we believe, also relevant to the way in which synods work in dioceses and deaneries.

9.2   Many of the criticisms made about synodical government are aimed not so much at it as a concept, but at how it is perceived to work in practice. The evidence we received contained a strong thread of concern about the impression which reports of General Synod meetings give of conflict and 'party' differences in the Church of England and the Synod as a body constantly racked by internal division. The expression of strong differences of view might be acceptable in the Westminster Parliament (although even there it sometimes seems forced and gratuitous) but, some of our correspondents urged, surely not in a Church bound together by a duty of Christian charity.

9.3   Linked with this criticism is another which questions whether the General Synod has adopted a form of procedure which too readily apes that of the Westminster Parliament. Allied with this is the suggestion that the representative character of synods misleadingly suggests that the government of the Church is about the application of principles of democracy (which it is not), and that the party or interest group system in the General Synod heightens the scope for and likelihood of internal dissension.

The purpose and conduct of a synod

9.4   We have set out in Chapter 2 our understanding of the theological basis of synodical government. It is clear from this that the purpose of a synod is to seek to understand God's will for the Church, and to engage representatives of all God's people in that task. A synod is emphatically not about the attempt to impose one group's view of what the Church should be on others.

9.5   While synodical government is built on the theological principle that all God's people should be represented in the government of the Church, it is not about democracy. Elections, debates and votes are simply mechanisms (imperfect human ones) which the Church uses to try to put the principle into action. Nor are they the only mechanisms.

9.6   Like all other aspects of Christian life, the first essential for a synod is that all its activities are grounded in prayer. That is why meetings of the General Synod and other synods already take place within a context of worship. Some members of Synod consider that sufficient; the Synod gathers to do business, not to pray. We believe that prayer and spirituality should be a thread running through the whole life of the Synod. An example of such a moment of prayer came during debate on 'The Church and the Bomb', in February 1983, and another before the final approval vote on the legislation on the ordination of women to the priesthood. Such pauses, which need not only precede voting, serve as a reminder that the shared task of Synod is to wait on God. **We recommend more imaginative use of pauses for prayer and quiet reflection during meetings of the General Synod.**

9.7   Synods should also seek to enhance and not undermine the unity of the Body of Christ. They are expected to reach decisions but they also have a reconciling task, in which the discernment of where consensus lies is more important than the views of majorities. Minorities are to be heard and in some senses protected. But how is this to be achieved in a world in which there are strongly held differences of view on key issues, and where decisions must be taken for the sake of the Church's mission? Does this mean that minorities must always be given a veto?

9.8   The answer to this latter question is 'no', although in some instances it may be appropriate for the majority to hold back on an issue at least for a period. What is right can only be judged in the circumstances of each issue, and it is one of the roles of synodical leaders (episcopal, clerical and lay) to make that judgement. Nor should vigorous debate between conflicting views be regarded as un-Christian; it has been a feature of the Christian Church since its earliest days and, far from being a sign of a Church in its death throes, is a sign of a Church full of energy and life.

9.9   Nevertheless the task of a synod is not limited to discerning where the majority view on an issue lies. It should be the aim in the conduct of any synodical business to maximise the area of agreement and minimise the area of disagreement. This takes time and effort. It is effort rewarded in the greater unity of the Church. Several of the present features of synodical government – votes by houses, special majorities, references of certain legislation to dioceses – are a recognition of the diversity of the Church and the need to build a sufficient basis of agreement on key issues. These are features which, although irksome to some in certain circumstances, are to be safeguarded.

9.10   Some might argue that the attempt to achieve consensus should be carried even further. The conduct of business at meetings of the Religious Society of Friends (the Quakers), for example, avoids (we understand) votes and seeks to form a 'mind of the meeting' through a mixture of discussion, prayer and reflection. This is an admirable and skilled process, and there may well be ways in which other Churches, including the Church of England, can learn from it. While, as we have said earlier, we believe there is more scope for prayer and reflection in the conduct of Synod business, we doubt that this could provide a way of avoiding continuing differences of view which, within a body as large as the General Synod (even on the reduced scale we propose), could only be settled by votes. There is nothing inherently un-Christian about deciding matters by vote, although the irony of the Legal Adviser heralding the General Synod's moment of decision with the instruction to 'Divide' has not escaped us. **We recommend that when a vote is taken it would be more appropriate for the Legal Adviser to call upon members to 'Vote!' than to 'Divide!'**

9.11   The key considerations are that:

*   the procedures leading up to a disputed decision are regarded as having been fairly conducted, with minorities having been

heard and a genuine attempt made to maximise the area of agreement; and

- the tone and style in which the discussion and vote are conducted avoid bitterness and rancour.

Individual synod members have a responsibility always to 'speak the truth in love' (Ephesians 4.15). It is when they become preoccupied with procedural point-scoring, or fixed on the truth as they see it to the exclusion of regard for others and their views, that honest disagreement becomes negative and divisive. In this context it is encouraging that following some highly contentious broadcast debates, the Secretary General of the General Synod has received a number of letters from members of the public expressing gratitude for the spirit in which the debate has been conducted.

9.12   Synod members need to demonstrate by their manner and attendance their commitment to a synod in which the contribution of all is recognised. We recognise that not every member is interested in every subject and that it would be impracticable to insist that all members be present for all debates. However, we have noticed the tendency of some members to vote without having heard a debate. This is familiar in Parliament but to be deprecated in Synod. We have considered whether fixed breaks for tea and coffee would be desirable in order to prevent members absenting themselves for this purpose, but think this would prove too disruptive to a General Synod sitting. However, we strongly deplore the practice of some members in arranging meetings during a sitting. When Synod is in session it should command the first loyalty of all members.

The Westminster model

9.13   One of the criticisms of the General Synod which we mentioned earlier is that its procedures are too closely modelled on those of the Westminster Parliament. This is partly directed at the adversarial style of the proceedings, on which we have just commented, but there are other elements in this criticism, viz.:

- that the procedures of Synod actually encourage conflict, because they are too closely based on those of Parliament; and

81

- that the Synod has also imported one of the least desirable features of Westminster, the 'party system'.

In considering this criticism we recognise the need to avoid generalising about the Westminster Parliament. Party political combat does not characterise all of the proceedings of the House of Commons, even less those of the House of Lords.

9.14   A basic function of the General Synod is to act, under the authority and scrutiny of Parliament, as the Church of England's legislature. Parliament has delegated to it certain of its responsibilities in this respect. The Synod has to demonstrate to Parliament and the world that ecclesiastical legislation has been at least as well considered by it as it would have been had it undergone full scrutiny in Parliament. It is understandable therefore that in its legislative capacity the Synod should model itself on the procedures of Parliament.

9.15   The Synod has other functions than the legislative, however. For example, it has to:

(a)   consider proposals for amendment of the Church's liturgy, a task in some ways similar to that of considering legislative proposals, in others not;

(b)   consider and approve budgets and other items of financial business;

(c)   debate other policy questions of general concern to the Church;

(d)   discuss and express a church view on issues of wider concern in society;

(e)   scrutinise the work of national church bodies, as a mechanism for ensuring their accountability.

In order to carry out each of these different tasks the Synod has developed and embodied in its Standing Orders a variety of procedures. These are regularly reviewed by the Standing Orders Committee of the Synod.

9.16   We have noticed in recent years a willingness on the part of the Standing Committee of the General Synod (which is responsible for putting together the Synod's agenda) to experiment with different ways of doing Synod business. These have included study of reports from the Doctrine Commission and from others in groups; the presentation of reports by representatives of groups affected using audio-visual means; and panel discussions including the opportunity for members to question the panel on key issues. **We welcome this more imaginative approach to the conduct of Synod's business, and we recommend that it be further extended.** It is, of course, essential when new processes are tried that they should not undermine confidence in existing good practice, and that all concerned should be very clear about what the new process or procedure is, how it is intended to operate, what its limits are and so on. Nevertheless the management of the business of a body like the General Synod requires constant re-evaluation. We hope that the new Business Committee of the General Synod (proposed as part of the follow-up to the Turnbull Report) will see this as one of its main, continuing responsibilities.

Groups in the Synod

9.17   Within the General Synod there are a range of different interest groups, which have developed informally over the years. Broadly speaking there have been three main groupings reflecting different strands of churchmanship: the catholic group, the evangelical group and the open synod group (which is sometimes described as the 'liberal group'). In fact this threefold division has never been very rigid, and since the enactment of the Priests (Ordination of Women) Measure it has become even less so. One of the features of the groups in Synod has always been that some members belong to more than one of them. This is one of many ways in which these groups differ from parties in the Westminster Parliament. Like the parties, the interest groups are complex and there are many divergences of view within them. The three broad groupings are increasingly fissiparous; for example, there are differences between traditional and affirming catholics and between traditional and progressive evangelicals. The crucial difference between them and the parliamentary parties is that they do not seek to exert discipline over their members. While they may, following discussion, seek to advise their members on how to vote on a particular issue, there is no system of 'whipping' to enforce a particular line. So to draw an analogy between groups in Synod and parties in Parliament is misleading and too simplistic.

9.18   The groupings reflect the fact that in one sense the Church of England itself is a coalition (as indeed are most if not all other churches). Within it are to be found different strands of churchmanship. These are united in a common profession of faith and share a liturgy and institutions in common, but differ in some respects in the way they seek to express their faith both in worship and in other ways. Interest groups in Synod reflect these wider differences of churchmanship. They have some positive features; for example they provide for their members a source of information and advice, a forum for discussion with generally like-minded people, and a means of mutual support. In this context, they are both an understandable and acceptable feature of the Synod. They become unacceptable when they set partisan concerns above the good of the wider Church. In the minds of all should be the admonition of St Paul to the Church at Corinth not to engage in party spirit (1 Corinthians 3).

The cost of the General Synod

9.19   Criticism of the way General Synod works is often linked with criticism of its cost. In fact the cost of meetings of the General Synod, while significant, is not unduly large. The cost per day of a meeting of the General Synod in London has been estimated at £29,000 and in York at £32,500 (based on 1996 prices), including subsistence costs. The cost of travel to the meetings is additional. These daily rates also exclude the cost of staff time to prepare for and service meetings. It would, however, be difficult to separate out that cost from the other activities of staff in support of the work of the Church at national level. The cost of the whole General Synod organisation in 1995 was just over £6 million; this includes the cost of all the national boards and councils of the Church. Even so this sum amounts to less than 1 per cent of the total cost of the Church of England, or only eleven pence on average from each adult church member per week. There is need for constant vigilance in order to keep costs generated by meetings of the Synod to the minimum compatible with the task to be done.

Frequency, timing and location of meetings

9.20   Until 1992 the General Synod used to meet three times a year. In other provinces of the Anglican Communion the provincial synod meets annually or even less. The fact that the Synod is engaged in framing legislation requires it, however, to meet reasonably often if the legislation before it is to go through all its stages in an acceptable space of time.

9.21   Nevertheless, in July 1992 the General Synod decided to try to reduce the frequency of its meetings from three to two a year (two being the minimum number required by the Synod's Constitution). It did so in response to concerns expressed by a number of dioceses about the level of the costs apportioned on dioceses. This move was widely welcomed by dioceses at the time.

9.22   In fact the Synod has been only partially successful in this resolve. It was recognised when the decision was taken that it might occasionally be necessary for the Synod to hold a shorter third meeting in certain years because of the need to deal with, for example, urgent legislative business. This proved to be the case in 1994 when Synod also met in February primarily to decide whether to promulge Canon C4B and Amending Canon No 13 relating to the ordination of women to the priesthood, and again in 1996 when Synod met to allow it to consider in particular draft legislation designed to enable the introduction of new arrangements for funding clergy pensions. Nevertheless the Synod did not meet in February 1995 or February 1997. In the period 1990–6 it met on a total of 74 days (in whole or in part), an average of 10.5 days a year.

9.23   The key point is that the Synod should not meet unless there is business which it alone can appropriately transact. This means that the Standing Committee (or the Business Committee under the proposed post-Turnbull arrangements) should scrutinise rigorously requests for matters to go before the Synod, whether these are demands for legislation or for reports or other work produced by the Church's boards and councils to be debated. The first question is whether a particular piece of work is essential. If it is, the second is whether it needs to absorb Synod time. Not all reports require debate in Synod. Again a flexible and imaginative approach is needed which ensures that full consideration is given (*before* work is commissioned) to whether it is necessary and how the outcome is to be handled. We believe that the proposed Archbishops' Council will have an important part to play in this regard.

9.24   At present Article 3 (1) of the Constitution of the General Synod provides that 'it shall meet in session at least twice a year.' We believe that the responsibility for deciding how often it meets should rest with the Synod itself, advised by the Standing (or in future the Business) Committee. That decision can only be taken in the light of the weight of business to be considered, measured against the key criterion set out in the preceding paragraph. The Synod must be ready to adjust its programme to meet shifting circumstances, and the wider Church must be willing to give it the freedom to discharge its responsibilities within the parameters we have described. Consistent with these considerations, the downward pressure on the number of meetings should be maintained. **We recommend therefore that the requirements of Article 3 (1) of the Constitution of the General Synod that it meet in session at least twice a year be repealed and that the Synod be free to determine the frequency of its own meetings.**

9.25   We have received some complaints about the timing of the General Synod's meetings. These presently take place during mid-week in November (and, if necessary, in February) and over a long weekend in July. Meetings held mid-week will discourage some lay people, particularly younger people, from standing for election to Synod, because they are unable to give up time from work. On the other hand many clergy are unwilling to be absent from their parishes at the weekend. While there are disadvantages to the present pattern of meetings, we believe most people accept them as a reasonable compromise. Certainly no one has, in evidence to us, suggested a better alternative.

9.26   The General Synod meets at the moment in Church House, Westminster in November (and, if necessary, February) and at the University of York in July. While some Synod members prefer one venue to the other, we believe that most appreciate the use of both venues and the way this involves both Provinces of the Church. Again we see the question of the location of its meetings as a matter for Synod itself to review from time to time, and **we make no recommendation ourselves for change.**

Detailed issues of procedure

9.27   The procedures of the General Synod are set out in its Standing Orders, which are kept under regular review by the Synod's Standing Orders Committee. During the quinquennium 1990–5, the Standing Orders were completely revised in an attempt to streamline and simplify them.

9.28   We do not think it our task to second-guess the Standing Orders Committee by reviewing all aspects of synodical procedure. Nevertheless some specific questions have been raised in evidence on which we think it appropriate to comment. These concern:

(a)   Diocesan synod motions;

(b)   Private members' motions;

(c)   Question time;

(d)   Voting by Houses and other special procedures.

(A)   Diocesan synod motions

9.29   Diocesan synod motions are passed by a diocesan synod with a request that they be debated in the General Synod. They may concern issues of Church or public policy (recent examples have included communion before confirmation and animal welfare). They may have far-reaching consequences (for example, the request for legislation to enable the ordination of women to the priesthood originated in the Diocese of Southwark). The motions may have originated in a PCC, and thereafter been endorsed at deanery and diocesan level before reaching the General Synod. As such, they represent an important means of enabling parishes and dioceses to influence the agenda of the national Church.

9.30   Diocesan synod motions will not necessarily always be best handled through a debate in the General Synod. The Standing Committee of the General Synod has discretion to decide when they can most opportunely be debated, and may from time to time suggest to a diocese that a motion be withdrawn because events have overtaken it. The consent of the submitting diocese is, however, rightly required to their withdrawal. **When a debate on a diocesan synod**

motion is appropriate, we recommend that it should be given a measure of priority over other business.

(B)   PRIVATE MEMBERS' MOTIONS

9.31   Under the General Synod's Standing Orders, members of Synod may table motions for debate on any issue. To be eligible for debate, a motion must be signed by at least 100 members over the course of three groups of sessions, otherwise it will lapse. Such motions are debated according to the number of signatures they attract. Generally speaking, at least one such motion is debated at every meeting of the Synod.

9.32   Some are very critical of this facility because such motions can force divisive issues to the top of the Church's agenda. Some see them as a charter for activists. For others they are an essential means of giving the General Synod the chance to debate issues of current concern in the Church, of keeping it in touch with the movement of opinion and of enabling individual 'back bench' Synod members to influence events.

9.33   We see force in both the criticisms of private members' motions and the argument for their retention. On balance, however, we do not believe that the present Standing Orders are effective to ensure that the General Synod's limited and valuable time for debate is only taken up by issues of real importance and concern to the Church. We think a more effective procedure for this purpose, **which we accordingly recommend, would be that a member of the General Synod wishing to raise an issue for debate should be required first to table the appropriate motion in his or her diocesan synod**, thus ensuring that a motion originated by a private member would only reach the General Synod if it had the endorsement of a diocesan synod.

(C)   QUESTION TIME

9.34   At meetings of the General Synod, questions may be addressed to the chairmen of the committees and commissions of the Synod (including its boards and councils), to the Secretary General, to the Financial Secretary and to the chairman of any Church of England body on which the Synod is represented. They may be answered orally or given a written answer. If answered orally, not only the questioner but any other member of Synod may ask one supplementary question each on the same topic.

9.35   The procedure is modelled on question time in Parliament but there the parallel ends. In particular the combative atmosphere of question time in the House of Commons is generally absent. Nevertheless some are critical of the spectacle of the Archbishop of Canterbury being subjected to challenging questioning, and regard it as demeaning to the Church and his office.

9.36   We do not agree with this criticism. Question time in Synod is an important means of enabling those who hold particular responsibilities in the Church to give an account of their stewardship and has a valuable role in helping to disseminate information on current issues. It is also another way in which individual Synod members may bring to notice the concerns of those they represent.

9.37   Nevertheless it is important that Synod members should not abuse the question-time procedure. It should never be an occasion for theological or partisan point-scoring, but should be used genuinely for the purpose of eliciting information. That is why the Standing Orders of the Synod should continue to exclude questions which are hypothetical or which seek to elicit an expression of opinion. We hope that members will also show restraint in how many questions are tabled for oral as against written answer, and in exercising their right to pose supplementary questions; and if they are answering questions, in the length of the answers given. If they do not, experience shows that frustration is the result. These are matters for the Synod's Business Committee to monitor rigorously.

9.38   The cost of answering questions in Synod has to be borne in mind and we have considered whether it is justified. On balance we believe that, for the reasons we have given earlier, it is. Nevertheless we believe that there should be some limit on the expense incurred in answering a question. We understand that current practice is, broadly speaking, to decline to answer a question if it will take more than one hour of staff time to prepare the answer. We endorse this as a sensible rule of thumb.

(D)   VOTING BY HOUSES AND OTHER SPECIAL PROCEDURES

9.39   The Constitution and Standing Orders of the General Synod lay down a number of special procedures such as the requirement that certain business should only be carried if it has been passed with majorities in all three Houses of the Synod, or if it has been approved by a majority of diocesan synods. Under Standing Order 36 (d) a division by Houses must be held, unless the Synod expressly decides otherwise, on final approval of any Measure or Canon, and may be held on any other question where the Chairman so orders or 25 members so request.

9.40   We have considered, in particular, the special procedures laid down by Article 8 of the Constitution of the General Synod. The text of Article 8 (1) is set out and its provisions are discussed in another context in paragraph 12.14 below where we welcome the procedure it prescribes and suggest that it may be appropriately applied more widely than the Article requires. Here we are only concerned to examine criticisms of Article 8.

9.41   Article 8 requires any Measure or Canon providing for permanent changes in the services of Baptism or Holy Communion or in the Ordinal, or a scheme for constitutional union or a permanent and substantial change of relationship between the Church of England and another Christian body, to be referred to diocesan synods before being finally approved by the General Synod. The business cannot be considered by the General Synod for final approval unless a majority of diocesan synods has approved the proposal. Under Article 8 as amended by the Synodical Government (Special Majorities) Measure 1971 a scheme of the kind referred to may also be required to be approved by such special majorities as may be specified in a resolution of the General Synod.

9.42   Any question whether Article 8 applies to a proposal, is to be conclusively determined by the Archbishops, the Prolocutors of the Convocations and the Chairman and Vice-Chairman of the House of Laity. In the early years of the life of the General Synod on a number of occasions legal advice as to whether business was or was not subject to Article 8 of the Constitution was rejected by the six Officers who, it was alleged, exercised a political judgement in the matter rather than a legal judgement.

9.43   It has been suggested by some that these decisions should be removed from the political arena by transferring the right to decide to, say, the Vicars General of the two Provinces who are ex-officio members of the Synod. The previous acrimonious discussions concerning the designation or non-designation of Article 8 business have not been heard for ten years or more and the precedents seem now to be well known and accepted by all. **We are therefore not minded to recommend any change in this provision.**

9.44   Some evidence we received argued that voting by Houses and other special procedures should be abandoned on the grounds that they were divisive and in conflict with the essentially consensual nature of a Synod.

9.45   Although such procedures may appear quaint or frustrating (depending on one's view of the particular issue under discussion), we believe that they are an essential part of the overall system of checks and balances within synodical government designed to ensure that, when issues which are central to the life of the Church are under discussion, the whole Church signifies its consent before change occurs. It is particularly important that the role of the bishops as guardians of the faith and doctrine of the Church, and the right of dioceses to be consulted on key changes, should be underpinned by such practical mechanisms. These are not merely procedural devices; their rationale is rooted in the theology and ecclesiology of the Church. **For these reasons, although we recognise that these procedures may sometimes be cumbersome and time-consuming, we recommend no change.**

10

The electoral system

The electoral basis

10.1   In this chapter, we consider the system of election employed at the various levels of synodical government. (The arrangements for the election of PCCs and our proposals at the deanery level are discussed in Chapters 4 and 5 and need no further elaboration.) We summarise the criticisms we have heard of the present system for elections to the General Synod and diocesan synods, particularly in relation to representatives of the laity, and we set out our proposals for change.

(a) The General Synod

(I) CLERGY

10.2   The system for electing representatives of the clergy to the General Synod has attracted little criticism, no doubt because the electorate in each diocese comprises all beneficed and licensed clergy. We believe it right that such clergy should continue to be eligible to vote and to stand for election, except that no person in episcopal orders should be an elector or be eligible to stand for election to the House of Clergy.

10.3   We propose one change which relates to retired clergy. It has been represented to us that on retirement they remain faithful members of the Church and that many of them continue to make an important (and growing) contribution to the active ministry. Yet they have no vote in elections to diocesan synods or the General Synod, nor may they stand for election to the General Synod. We share the concern that this valued and substantial group of people should be subject to these disabilities. We believe that representatives of retired clergy with permission to officiate should be eligible to vote and stand in elections to the General Synod, but that measures should be in place to ensure that the views of the active clergy are not swamped by those of their retired colleagues. **We therefore recommend that 10** per cent of the retired clergy in each diocese with permission to officiate should be elected by their peers as electors to the House of Clergy of the General Synod and that all retired clergy with permission to officiate should be eligible to stand as candidates for election.

(II) LAITY

10.4   We propose no change to the present principle by which seats are allocated to each diocese, to be filled by election in the diocese. There is, however, a widespread belief that the deanery synod has not generally provided a satisfactory electorate for the House of Laity. Because deanery synods are thought to be irrelevant by many church members, attracting candidates to stand for election to them is sometimes difficult and elections are often uncontested. Moreover, deanery synods have a wide range of functions. Those offering themselves for election may have varied and valuable experience, but their primary interests may not lie in the exercise of the franchise at elections for the General Synod and diocesan synods. That may be a contributing factor to the further criticisms we have encountered to the effect that the views of the parishes are not adequately represented at the General Synod and that in many parishes little is known about those elected to represent them.

10.5   Our proposal that the deanery synod should no longer form a unit of synodical government imposes on us a requirement to establish a new electoral basis for elections to General Synod and to diocesan synods. But even if deanery synods were to be retained as a continuing level of synodical government, we would not consider it desirable that they should retain their electoral function.

10.6   In seeking to devise an alternative electoral arrangement we have had two main objectives in view. First, to establish a system which will enable parishes to have a direct involvement in the electoral process and so to feel confidence in its outcome. Secondly, to establish an electorate who will exercise the franchise responsibly to ensure, as far as may be, that the wishes of the parishes are accurately reflected. In this way we hope to ensure that parishes may have confidence in those elected to represent them, and that those elected are well equipped to represent their constituents in the wider counsels of the Church.

10.7   We have considered carefully whether these objectives might be best achieved by a system of universal suffrage, with a vote in elections to the diocesan synod and the General Synod for every person whose name is on an electoral roll. Those advocating this approach argue that the General Synod would be more credible in the eyes of both Church members and others if individual laity could vote directly for those who are to represent them on it. They also argue that direct elections, coupled with universal suffrage, are the only method acceptable in a modern democratic society. Whilst recognising that electoral rolls are an imperfect measure of church membership, they suggest that if inclusion on an electoral roll is the sole qualification for participation in the electoral process at all levels of synodical government, those who fail to join the roll will have only themselves to blame if they are displeased with the outcome of elections.

10.8   These considerations are weighty and we have some sympathy for them. However, there are also weighty considerations which point in a different direction. Analogies cannot be safely drawn from parliamentary elections. General Synod elections have little to compare with the overwhelming media coverage at general elections which does so much to ensure a high level of participation by the voters. It is significant that turn-outs are much lower for local authority elections. We have seen little evidence of a widespread desire within the parishes for universal participation in Synod elections; on the contrary, the indications are that the percentages among those participating in the elections would be so low as to undermine any claim by the successful candidates to have secured a strong measure of grass roots support.

10.9   Further, the organisation of effective hustings aimed at a churchwide electorate would present considerable difficulties. Electors would not find it easy to inform themselves of the merits of the candidates, and we believe that a growing tendency would emerge for elections to be fought on party lines. That is not a trend we should wish to encourage.

10.10   None of this is to say that there is a total absence of interest in parishes in the composition and work of the General Synod. But in general we believe that, while many parishioners might welcome an opportunity to express their views in broad terms, they would be glad to entrust to others the translation of those views into effective votes if the means of doing so were available.

10.11 Finally, we see considerable practical difficulty and cost in organising elections on the basis of universal suffrage which could be depended upon to be free of significant irregularity. Our enquiries suggest that the cost, excluding staff time, for a diocese with some 50,000 names on its electoral rolls would probably be in the order of £50,000 to £60,000, a total of about £1.5 million for the Church as a whole. We believe that there would be great reluctance in the Church to incur that sort of expenditure on a system as seriously flawed as we consider universal suffrage exercised in the context we have described would turn out to be.

10.12 An alternative approach which has its adherents would be to make the elected lay members of the diocesan synod the electorate for General Synod. This would have the merit of providing an informed electorate, knowledgeable about most of the candidates standing for election. But it has the major disadvantage of failing to satisfy our first objective that parishes should have a direct involvement in the electoral process. Many parishes are not represented directly on the diocesan synod (nor, as we explain in paragraph 10.22, do we think it practicable for them to be so) and to have the General Synod elected by the diocesan synod would do nothing to narrow the gap between General Synod and parish that is one of the most common criticisms of the present system.

10.13 We wish to commend a different approach. **We recommend that each parish should elect at its annual parochial church meeting a number of lay people, to be known as synodical electors, who would form the electors for the lay members of the General Synod and the diocesan synod; each parish should elect one elector for each 50 members, or part thereof, on its electoral roll.** This would ensure that every parish had a direct interest in the electoral process, while providing a suitable weighting in approximate proportion to the number of electoral roll members. Taken together with the recommendation in the next paragraph, it would create a total electorate approximating in size to the current membership of deanery synods. At present the lay members of deanery synods, as well as electing the lay members of the diocesan synod and of the General Synod, are themselves eligible to stand for election to either. We see no reason why the same should not apply to the synodical electors whom we propose.

10.14 Powers exist under Rule 27 of the Church Representation Rules for the diocesan synod to provide for the representation on a deanery synod of lay persons who are on the cathedral roll of a parish church cathedral, or who are declared by the dean of any other cathedral to be habitual worshippers at the cathedral church and whose names are not entered on the electoral roll of any parish. **We recommend that these powers should be amended to provide in like terms for the election of synodical electors by cathedral worshippers.**

10.15 Those chosen to serve as electors would have as their key task the casting of votes in elections to the General Synod and to the diocesan synod. They would not be members of the PCC ex-officio, but should be invited to be present, if not otherwise a member, at PCC meetings when election issues are being discussed. They would be expected to inform themselves, by this and whatever other means might be most appropriate to the circumstances of their parishes, of the views of the parishioners on the issues to be dealt with in the new synod and the sort of candidates considered to be best able to tackle such issues.

10.16 They would also be expected to inform themselves about the candidates standing for election. As part of this process we see it as important that electors should attend meetings with candidates to ascertain their views on the issues facing the Church. Electors who were freed from attending other meetings (unless they voluntarily undertook other duties) and whose sole responsibility was the exercise of the franchise on behalf of their parishes might be expected to give a much sharper sense of purpose to hustings.

10.17 All of this would impose a greater obligation on candidates to make themselves and what they stand for widely known to the electors. Further, it would, we believe, encourage a measure of reporting back and communication during the lifetime of a Synod. But we would expect this to be welcomed as a means of bringing greater reality to the effective representation of the whole Church in the synodical system. A major criticism of the present system has been its remoteness from the lives of ordinary parishioners. Nothing is likely to remove that entirely, but we hope that our proposals will make a valuable contribution to the narrowing of what we believe to be an unacceptably wide gulf between General Synod and parish pew.

10.18   It is clearly important that the register of synodical electors should be as up to date as possible at the time of each election. We therefore propose that its members should be elected each year at the annual parochial church meeting, all those on the electoral roll being eligible to vote.   Annual election of synodical electors should not imply frequent changes in the electorate. A considerable measure of continuity would clearly be desirable, with those elected being normally expected to see through at least one electoral cycle of the General Synod.

10.19   We do not support a proposal put to us that an upper age limit should be introduced for lay members seeking election to synodical office. A significant percentage of those who are active in the life of the Church are above the normal retirement age. These people should not be excluded from active involvement in Church government. The year of birth already appears on voting papers and it should be left to the discretion of the electorate whether older lay members are elected.

(b) Diocesan synods

(I)   CLERGY

10.20   We see no need for change in the basis of election to the house of clergy of diocesan synods, save that the recommendations we make in paragraph 10.3 above would also apply to these elections. **The number of clergy to be elected should continue to be determined by resolution of the outgoing diocesan synod, being based on the number of beneficed and licensed clergy in each deanery.**

(II)   LAITY

10.21   We have recommended in paragraph 10.13 that synodical electors should constitute the electorate for the house of laity in the diocesan synod as well as in the General Synod. We do not otherwise propose changes in the arrangements for elections to diocesan synods. The number of laity to be elected should continue to be determined by resolution of the outgoing diocesan synod, being based on the total number on the electoral rolls of the parishes in each deanery within the limits to which we refer in paragraph 6.10 above. As now, any communicant lay person whose name was on an electoral roll of a parish in the deanery would be eligible to be elected to the diocesan synod, and voting would be by deaneries. Arrangements would also cover cathedral worshippers (see paragraph 10.14 above).

10.22 We recognise the tension between calls for direct representation from each parish on the diocesan synod and the need for the synod not to be so large as to inhibit useful debate and effective decision-making. Our conclusion is that direct representation must be ruled out on the grounds which we have already rehearsed. We believe that, certainly in the larger dioceses, one lay member from each parish would make for unwieldy synods, and we doubt whether a single member from each parish, regardless of its size, would constitute an acceptable basis of representation. If wider consultation is required the bishop can call a diocesan conference as provided for in the 1969 Measure (see paragraph 6.3 above).

Method of election

10.23 We set out in Appendix IV the background to the adoption by the General Synod of the 'single transferable vote' method of election. **For the reasons given there, we recommend its retention.** It is at present for dioceses to decide whether elections to diocesan synods should be by single transferable vote or the first past the post method of election. **We recommend that dioceses should retain their discretion in this matter.**

11

The General Synod and Parliament

11.1   The relationship between the General Synod and Parliament is potentially a very large subject. The historical note which appears at Appendix I contains a brief account of how the government of the Church of England has developed from Tudor times, when the Sovereign was, in substance as well as in name, the Church's Supreme Governor, through the period when Parliament was the sole author of all ecclesiastical legislation, down to the present century in which there has evolved the system we know today. Under that system the General Synod is the primary and normally the only originator of ecclesiastical legislation, although Parliament, of course, retains the power to originate and carry through legislation in the ecclesiastical, as in any other, field by Act of Parliament.

11.2   The General Synod legislates either by Measure or by Canon (Acts of Synod, in that they have no legally binding force, are not, in the strict sense of the word, legislation). Legislation by Canon, which is under the sole control of the General Synod, is now possible in large areas of concern, particularly in relation to the Church's forms of worship, which were once the subject of acute parliamentary controversy. But legislation by Canon is only possible for defined purposes. Hence there remain other important areas where legislative change in the status quo can only be effected by Measure. A Measure, having been passed by General Synod, still requires approval by resolution of both Houses of Parliament before it may be presented for the Royal Assent, the grant of which gives it the force and effect of an Act of Parliament.

11.3   In the pluralist society of England at the end of the twentieth century it is probably true to say that only a minority of Members of Parliament are active members of the Church of England. Seeing this to be so, many find it strange and anomalous that Parliament should still be in a position to veto legislation relating to the Church's organisation and operations which the Church's own legislature has approved. This is particularly so in matters which appear to concern the Church and its members alone. Good examples of this have been the two most controversial Measures of recent times, both concerned with the question of who may be ordained in the Church of England to the priesthood, the Clergy (Ordination) Measure 1990 and the Priests (Ordination of Women) Measure 1993. Both these Measures eventually secured the approval of both Houses of Parliament, but both were the subject of long and hotly contested debates in the Ecclesiastical Committee of Parliament. Indeed the former was initially rejected by the House of Commons at a sparsely attended sitting in the early hours of the morning and had to be the subject of a renewed motion for approval in the following parliamentary session.

11.4   On the other hand there are some matters for which it is appropriate for the Church to legislate but which do not concern the Church alone. To take only one example, legislation relating to the future of redundant churches is clearly of concern to all who value the nation's architectural heritage whatever their religion may be. There are many aspects of the national life in which the Church of England, as the national Church, has throughout its history occupied a position from which it must both be concerned with, and in which its activities must in turn affect and influence, a range of interests stretching far beyond the purely ecclesiastical. This position has been implicitly recognised by statute in that the authority which the General Synod exercises under the Church of England Assembly (Powers) Act 1919 (the 1919 Act) to legislate by Measure is limited only by section 3 (6) which provides that 'a Measure may relate to any matter concerning the Church of England.' This limitation is, in practice, so wide that, without some fundamental change in the constitutional basis on which synodical government presently rests, it is inevitable that Parliament should retain its powers of veto over a subordinate legislative body whose legislative authority would otherwise be of such large and imprecise scope.

11.5   The question of whether Parliament's voice in purely ecclesiastical affairs, which some resent, should be restrained and whether some fundamental legislative change in the nature of the powers delegated to the General Synod is called for are inextricably linked and are bound up with the whole question of the established character of the Church of England.

11.6   Our terms of reference, however, with respect to the relationship between the General Synod and Parliament are very narrow. Our review of the system set up by the 1969 Measure is required only to have 'particular reference to . . . communications . . . with Parliament.' The only formal communication between the General Synod and Parliament is through the machinery pursuant to the 1919 Act governing the procedure to be followed before a Measure which has been passed by the General Synod may obtain the required approval of both Houses of Parliament that it be presented for the Royal Assent. Thus, whereas the question of the relationship between, and the different functions exercised by, Parliament and the General Synod with respect to the government of the Church is very wide, the question of the communications between the two institutions is narrow and somewhat technical. It is this narrow question which we have addressed.

11.7   The 1919 Act prescribes the constitution and functions of the Ecclesiastical Committee, a joint committee of both Houses of Parliament, and it is through this body that all formal communications between the General Synod and Parliament are channelled. A paper on the Ecclesiastical Committee which has been prepared for us by Lord Bridge of Harwich has examined in some detail, first, the constitution and functions designed for the Committee by the framers of the 1919 legislation and how these were substantially transformed in the passage through Parliament of the Bill which became the Act of 1919, and, secondly, how the Committee has in practice operated, particularly in recent years and in relation to the more controversial Measures. We publish this paper as Appendix V to our report.

11.8   As appears from Appendix V, the framers of the 1919 legislation, in proposing to establish the Ecclesiastical Committee with a membership of Privy Councillors, intended that its primary function should be to subject legislation passed by the Church Assembly to highly qualified expert scrutiny in order to ensure that it was accurately drafted to achieve its ecclesiastical purposes and also that it did not bring about any unintended or untoward consequences affecting adversely interests other than those of the Church of England. Under the 1919 Act, as a result of amendments to the Bill made by the House of Commons, members of the Ecclesiastical Committee are members of the House of Commons and of the House of Lords nominated by the Speaker and the Lord Chancellor respectively. It appears to have been thought in 1919 that the members of the Committee would be selected as representing a variety of different interests, particularly those of non-conformist bodies. This may have been what happened in the early years of the life of the Ecclesiastical Committee, but it has certainly not been the practice in recent years, when the membership of the Committee has been almost entirely composed of members of the Church of England who take an active interest in its affairs. Not surprisingly, differences of opinion on matters of controversy in the Church are reflected among the members of the Committee and, before the Committee reports to Parliament on any controversial Measure, the issues which have been fully debated in the General Synod are likely to have been debated afresh by the Committee.

11.9   It is perhaps open to question whether the intermediate layer of debate in the Ecclesiastical Committee directed to issues which have been resolved by the General Synod before a Measure is passed, and which both Houses of Parliament will consider when they are asked to approve the Measure, makes a valuable or necessary contribution to the legislative process. It is clearly necessary that any Measure before it is submitted to both Houses for approval should be subject to scrutiny and report by some independent and suitably qualified body to ensure that it does not extend beyond the sphere in which the Church can properly be permitted to legislate and that it does not adversely affect civil rights or legitimate secular interests. It might well be possible, in the light of experience, to devise a body with a different constitution and different statutory functions from those laid down by the 1919 Act for the Ecclesiastical Committee which would provide the necessary safeguards more effectively and more expeditiously. But this could only be achieved by a new Act of Parliament in place of the 1919 Act.

11.10   We are aware that some in Parliament may themselves favour amendment of that Act so as to increase rather than lessen the opportunity for Members of Parliament to involve themselves in the detail of ecclesiastical legislation. Those who might take this view would assert Parliament's right to intervene in the affairs of the established Church and find the inability of the Ecclesiastical Committee of Parliament itself to amend draft Measures irksome. We do not however believe that there is any general appetite in Parliament to amend the 1919 Act, and indeed the arguments which led Parliament to delegate legislative authority in ecclesiastical matters to the Church Assembly and its successor the General Synod seem to us still to hold good. Moreover we are certain that any attempt fundamentally to shift the balance embodied in the 1919 Act in Parliament's favour would be vigorously resisted by the Church.

11.11   We are satisfied that no consideration falling within our terms of reference would justify a recommendation that any attempt should be made to modify the statutory framework under the 1919 Act which presently governs communications between the General Synod and Parliament. The system may not be perfect, but for practical purposes it functions reasonably well. It is always possible that some future government will introduce radical legislation to alter the present relations of Church and State or that some interest group will seek to do so. The Church will have to meet that situation if and when it arises. But for the Church to take the initiative in seeking to promote new primary legislation unless and until it has some important and clearly defined objective to pursue would be likely to create more problems than it would solve.

11.12   We have been pleased to learn that, during the passage of the recent Pensions Measure, informal conversations were held between Synod representatives and parliamentarians chaired by the Second Church Estates Commissioner with the aim of ensuring that the views of interested peers and MPs were fully understood and could be taken into account before the legislation reached its final form. We understand that similar conversations are envisaged in relation to the current draft National Institutions Measure. We believe that informal contacts of this nature are greatly to be encouraged and we hope that in future they may extend to other areas of common concern. Informal consultation on these lines seems to us to offer the best prospect that the Act of 1919 can be operated with a degree of flexibility without the need to disturb the delicate balance between Parliament and the Church which the Act embodies.

12

Communications

12.1   Our terms of reference require us to review the system of synodical government with particular reference to communications between the different levels. Even had they not done so, the evidence we received would have compelled us to look closely at this issue. Many submissions referred to the need for better communication between all levels of church government. There was a widespread feeling that present arrangements are inadequate, that there should be more consultation with those affected before key decisions are taken, and that communication must be two-way, with opportunity for parishes to influence and even set diocesan and General Synod agendas and not simply to be talked at from on high.

12.2   It is easier to make generalised requests for better communication than to offer specific practical suggestions for improvement. Some of the evidence we received suggested dissatisfaction less with the adequacy of communication than with the substance of decisions taken. There are various distinct strands to this issue. We need to remember that members of synodical bodies, whether of the PCC or of the General Synod, are elected to exercise their own judgement on the issues set before them, not simply to do their electors' bidding. But they are also to represent, as widely as possible, those who elected them, not to pursue narrow sectional interests. We need to be realistic in assessing just how much real appetite for more involvement in some of the issues there is in the average person in the pew. And we must bear in mind that all systems of government require the exercise of a degree of trust between those represented and those they choose to serve them. In the Church, in particular, trust should not be a commodity in short supply, but it has to be earned.

12.3   All this said, the evidence we received confirms our own belief that there is an unhealthy gap between synodical bodies and those they are supposed to represent. There is a widespread and reasonable demand to be better informed, to be consulted before decisions affecting particular groups or individuals are taken, and for those in positions of responsibility to be more readily accountable for their stewardship to those they serve. Openness, listening and accountability are demanded. These demands are likely to increase as the burden of financing the Church falls increasingly on the parishes.

12.4   In the remainder of this chapter we consider the contribution which all in the Church can make to improving communication flows. We emphasise 'all' because this is not a responsibility just of 'them' but of 'us.' Moreover we need to be realistic. There is no single 'quick-fix' solution. Rather the problem requires working at continuously and in a number of different ways.

The contribution of representatives

12.5   Members at all levels of synodical government have a responsibility to:

*   make clear their views on key issues when they seek election. At the parish level, most people (though not necessarily all) know each other reasonably well. At other levels, more formal devices like hustings and election addresses are required. Some election addresses are models of clarity, others of obfuscation. Electors have a right to know where those seeking their vote stand on key issues;

*   consult those they represent on major matters. There are various devices for this although we accept that the larger the constituency, the more difficult it becomes;

*   brief themselves well before meetings. As regards General Synod members it can often help if they meet together in their diocese in advance of the group of sessions to consider the agenda (perhaps with the help of their diocesan secretary);

*   report back to their constituents after meetings, either orally or (perhaps preferably) in writing. A number of members produce brief personal accounts of General Synod or diocesan synod meetings, for example, for distribution at deanery synods or PCCs. If oral reports are given, it is important to ensure that they are taken seriously and not constantly driven off the agenda by other business. We encourage dioceses to consider

helping people to report back in appropriate ways by providing suitable training.

The contribution of those represented

12.6   Those who are represented are not merely passive spectators but have an active part to play too in ensuring effective communication. Too often an alleged failure to communicate turns out to be a failure to read, or to listen to what is said. Those represented should create and take advantage of opportunities to question those who represent them. There can sometimes be a collusiveness in a parish, for example, which suggests that it is 'bad form' to probe issues too deeply at a PCC or an annual parochial church meeting. Openness needs to be a cherished part of every parish's culture and not simply something demanded of the diocese or the Church at national level.

The contribution of institutions

12.7   Effective communications do not simply happen, however, as a consequence of the interaction, however lively, between representatives and those they represent. The institutions of the Church – at all levels – need to develop positive policies for informing people of what is happening and consulting them (before decisions are taken) on proposals which affect them directly. The Church's approach to communications is still too often reactive rather than proactive. Every institution – from PCC to General Synod, and in due course the proposed Archbishops' Council – should reflect from time to time on how it can improve communication and consultation with those it seeks to serve. Simply exhorting people to communicate more effectively is not enough. Material and opportunities need to be provided to help the process, though with due recognition of what that may imply in terms of resources of money and people.

12.8   There are already a number of examples of good practice which might be extended or adopted in other areas. Many elected members of the General Synod are allocated responsibility for reporting back to specified deaneries in their diocese. Some produce, as we have noted, news-sheets or written personal reports to circulate.

Diocesan newspapers include items on diocesan synod debates. The Communications Unit of the General Synod produces a twice-yearly Update covering the work of the General Synod boards and councils and, as an experiment, recently produced a 15-minute audio tape of the highlights of a Synod meeting. There is an excellent privately produced written digest of the General Synod's meetings which a number of dioceses purchase and circulate widely. As regards consultation, there is regular consultation between the General Synod and dioceses, and between dioceses and parishes, on financial matters. Other major policy developments are also the subject of formal or informal reference.

12.9   Nonetheless there is an urgent requirement to develop these and other means of communication and consultation further. An obvious current gap (which we understand is in the process of being filled) is the lack of a short readable, annual report on the work of all the Church's national bodies, which can be made available widely in parishes. Such publications require skill and resources to produce. If we demand good communications, we ought also to recognise that they will not be provided without cost.

12.10   The Church should also be looking to exploit the latest developments in communications technology, including the Internet. These provide means through which information can potentially be disseminated widely to parishes and to individual church-goers. A number of dioceses and other church bodies are already experimenting with the use of such media. Again we urge that the Church adopt a strategic and proactive approach, so that resources and learning can be pooled and best practice extended.

12.11   As we noted earlier, good communications are not simply about passing information down from General Synod to diocese and parish; they should encourage a two-way flow. Along with informing and consulting there has also to be listening. We have reviewed our earlier recommendations with this in mind. Are they likely to encourage or impede a greater sense of ownership of the synodical process in parishes? We believe they will encourage it.

12.12   We have sought to embody in our proposals principles of transparency, accountability and subsidiarity. We have sought to simplify, clarify and increase the scope for the flexible adaptation of

institutions at each level to suit local circumstances. Thus our recommendation to remove deaneries from the straitjacket of the synod
system should, we believe, enable dioceses and parishes to design
means of co-operation which best meet their needs. Having electors
in each parish who will be informed about issues at diocesan and
General Synod level should, we believe, help increase accountability
through interchange with elected representatives. Ensuring that
General Synod members have to take motions through their diocesan
synod before they can go to the General Synod should help ensure
that the views they express are more fully reflective of those they
represent.

12.13   Some may be tempted to claim that our proposals to abolish
the deanery synod or to cut down the size of the General Synod are
likely to reduce effective communication because there will in future
be fewer elected members around to act as a channel of accountability. This is to slip into assuming that elected representatives are the
only or chief means of communication and accountability, and that
the more you have of them the better. We do not wish to understate
the role of elected representatives but we do ask for honesty in assessing it and a willingness to recognise that they are one important, but
not the only, means of maintaining confidence between the parishes
and those in positions of leadership and responsibility at diocesan
and national level.

12.14   It will be important that the Archbishops' Council proposed
by the Turnbull Report and to be constituted by the draft National
Institutions Measure presently before the General Synod ensures that
it carries dioceses with it as it seeks 'to co-ordinate, support and
generally further the work and mission of the Church of England'
(section 1 (1) of the draft Measure). There is already provision in
Article 8 (1) of the Constitution of the General Synod that:

> 'A Measure or Canon providing for permanent changes
> in the Services of Baptism or Holy Communion or in the
> Ordinal, or a scheme for a constitutional union or a
> permanent and substantial change of relationship
> between the Church of England and another Christian
> body, being a body a substantial number of whose
> members reside in Great Britain, shall not be finally

approved by the General Synod unless, at a stage determined by the Archbishops, the Measure or Canon or scheme, or the substance of the proposals embodied therein, has been approved by a majority of the dioceses at meetings of their Diocesan Synods, or, in the case of the diocese of Europe, of the bishop's council and standing committee of that diocese.'

We believe that this provision should remain. We hope that the proposed Archbishops' Council and the Business Committee will consider referring to dioceses other appropriate matters on which a formal reference under Article 8 is not statutorily required. We welcome, for instance, the decision to invite dioceses to consider and respond to the draft National Institutions Measure before it is considered further by the General Synod. We do not believe, however, that it is appropriate (or possible) to seek to prescribe what those matters should be. We would expect nonetheless that the Council and Committee will consider regularly whether a particular matter is one on which the views of dioceses should be sought.

12.15   We are conscious that in this chapter we have only scratched the surface of a large subject on which others may be far better equipped to pronounce. We do not, however, think it is one best tackled through pronouncements or exhortations handed down from on high. We are pleased to see that the importance of the issue has already been recognised at the national level in the development of the proposed Archbishops' Council. We hope that all those involved in the government of the Church at every level will be alive to their responsibility for effective communication.

13

Summary of conclusions and recommendations

13.1   Whilst we have encountered many detailed criticisms of the way in which synodical government in the Church of England operates, we have found overwhelming acceptance of the principles it embodies. Although there are some who would wish to abolish all synods, leaving the government of the Church solely in the hands of the bishops, the co-operation of representative clergy and laity with bishops in the running of the Church is widely valued, not only for the theological reasons we have discussed in Chapter 2, but also for the way in which it can be a means to mobilise effectively the resources and goodwill of the whole Church in the service of the Gospel.

13.2   At the same time the operation of synodical government is frequently associated with some of the less attractive aspects of bureaucracy: a proliferation of paper and committees, and the stifling of individual responsibility and initiative. There is a widespread ignorance of the way in which synodical government works at its different levels, but there is significant and justified complaint about some of its features, especially at the level of the deanery synod.

13.3   We hope that our report will help to dispel some of the ignorance about synodical government and provide a basis on which to evaluate some of the wilder criticisms of it. Many of these are an example of criticising the messenger rather than the message, of complaining about the machinery or processes of synodical government when the actual object of the criticism is some decision or other which those elected to represent us have taken. Similarly the right response to many criticisms is not to tinker with structures or organisation but to change how we work them.

13.4   Nonetheless a number of the criticisms made in evidence to us are justified and our recommendations for change seek to address them. These are listed below. We have tried to ensure that our proposals are true to the theological principles we discussed in Chapter 2 and suit the contemporary context we described in Chapter 3. We believe that they affirm principles of openness, accountability, and subsidiarity. We have sought to lighten the burden, to prescribe only where necessary, and to leave the maximum scope for the exercise of local discretion consistent with having a national framework for the Church's government. Where something is working well, we have recommended leaving it alone. We believe that, taken together, our recommendations will strengthen confidence in the operation of synodical government and in that hope we commend them for consideration.

13.5   In the following paragraphs we set out a brief summary of our general conclusions with respect to the operation of synodical government at each different level and of our proposal for the reform of the electoral system. We then set out our positive recommendations for change *seriatim* under each heading. Our reasons for making each recommendation are explained in the relevant paragraphs of the earlier chapters.

The parish

13.6   In general we have concluded that the existing system works well at the parish level and that only minor changes are called for in the provisions of the Church Representation Rules relating to the membership of the PCC and in certain provisions relating to conventional districts. Our detailed recommendations are:

- that provision should be included in Rule 10 (1) that candidates shall not be eligible for election to a PCC unless their names have been on the electoral roll for a period of at least twelve months (see paragraph 4.14).

- that Rule 16 (1) be amended so that the system of election under the proviso, which now only operates if the annual meeting so decides, be prescribed for all PCCs, with the effect that lay members will be elected for a three-year term and a third of them will retire annually in rotation but be eligible for re-election (see paragraph 4.16).

111

- that Rule 14 (1) (g) should be amended to provide that, unless the annual parochial meeting determines otherwise, the number of lay representatives to be elected to the PCC should be nine plus three additional representatives for each 100 members (or part thereof) on the electoral roll over 100 (see paragraph 4.21).

- that conventional districts should be removed from the definition of 'parish' in the Church Representation Rules (see paragraph 4.39).

- that in any conventional district there should be a review of the pastoral situation by the bishop and the diocesan pastoral committee at five-yearly intervals (see paragraph 4.40).

The deanery

13.7   There is much dissatisfaction with the existing system of synodical government at the deanery level, albeit not with deaneries as such. It is important that groups of parishes should be able to work together in many ways in furtherance of the Church's mission and suitable arrangements need to be in place to make that co-operation effective. But we have concluded that the statutory deanery synod is not always, or even generally, the best institution to achieve that objective and that dioceses should be free to devise arrangements best suited to local circumstances which vary so greatly as between different parts of the country and indeed within individual dioceses. Our detailed recommendations are:

- that the statutory requirement for deanery synods to be part of the formal structure of synodical government should be repealed (see paragraph 5.19).

- that each diocese should be required to produce a scheme or schemes for deanery arrangements to be approved by the diocesan synod and which should be subject to review every five years (see paragraph 5.20).

- that the diocesan determination of deanery arrangements should be strengthened by the repeal of the present provisions in the Pastoral Measure 1983 which require a pastoral scheme or order to be made by the Church Commissioners before a deanery boundary can be altered, and the enactment of provisions allowing the primary decision with respect to the alteration of deanery boundaries by the re-allocation of parishes within deaneries to be made by the diocesan synod so as to effect the grouping of parishes most suitable to local needs. If this recommendation is accepted, it will be necessary to provide a right for any parish objecting to a re-allocation proposed by the diocese to appeal to some independent body (see paragraph 5.21).

The diocese

13.8   Here again we have encountered no major criticism of the existing system as it operates at diocesan level. There is no single theme running through Chapter 6 of our report, but we propose a number of minor changes, including some which are consequential on our recommendations in relation to deaneries. Our detailed recommendations are:

- that there should be added to the statutory functions of a diocesan synod the following:

    (i)   to approve the annual budget and to receive the annual accounts for the diocese;

    (ii)   to approve arrangements for the effective operation of deaneries;

    (iii)   to keep deaneries and parishes informed of the policies and problems of the diocese, of the issues the diocesan synod is to consider and of the decisions it takes, and to receive and, where necessary, to take action on matters referred to it from deaneries and parishes (see paragraph 6.6).

- that Rule 31 (8) of the Church Representation Rules be amended to provide that the minimum number of members of a diocesan synod should be reduced to 100, and that each diocese should review the size of its diocesan synod taking account of the reality of the falling numbers of clergy, and of laity registered on the electoral rolls of parishes (see paragraph 6.10).

- that dioceses should be encouraged to review their arrangements for the membership of their bishop's council in the light of whatever pattern emerges at the national level (see paragraph 6.23).

- that the DBF, when it continues to operate as a distinct body, should be subordinate to the resolutions of the diocesan synod and that the Diocesan Board of Finance Measure 1925 be amended or replaced to remove existing doubts about the legality of establishing a single body to perform the functions of both the diocesan synod and the DBF and otherwise so as to provide flexibility for dioceses to make arrangements for the conduct of their financial business which best suit their circumstances (see paragraph 6.30).

- that paragraph 10 of Schedule I to the Pastoral Measure 1983 be amended so as to remove the requirement that a majority of members of a sub-committee appointed by the diocesan pastoral committee shall be members of that committee (see paragraph 6.34)

- that the Pastoral Measure 1983 be amended to provide that, where the diocesan synod so resolves, the functions of the diocesan redundant churches uses committee under section 42 may be performed by the diocesan pastoral committee or by any sub-committee thereof to whom any relevant function may be delegated under paragraph 10 of Schedule I of the 1983 Measure and that, so long as such a resolution is in force, the proceedings of the redundant churches uses committee shall be suspended (see paragraph 6.35).

- that statutory provision should be made which will give the diocesan secretary a legal persona but which will also allow dioceses themselves to allocate to the secretary such functions as they deem appropriate (see paragraph 6.39).

The Convocations

13.9   We have concluded that the Convocations no longer perform a necessary or useful legislative function and that their valuable deliberative and consultative function can be performed equally well and more economically by informal *ad hoc* meetings of the representative clergy of each Province. Our detailed recommendations are:

- that the provisions of Article 7 (2) to (6) of the Constitution of the General Synod be repealed and replaced by a simple requirement, similar to that formerly contained in the Constitution of the Church Assembly, that any legislative provision 'touching doctrinal formulae or the services or ceremonies of the Church of England or the administration of the sacraments or sacred rites thereof' shall be debated and voted upon by each of the three Houses of the General Synod sitting separately (see paragraph 7.9).

- that the Convocations should cease to exist; and that, in consequence, the suffragan bishops elected to the House of Bishops and the members of the House of Clergy of the General Synod should be directly elected on the same basis, subject to the changes recommended in Chapter 8, as that which presently governs elections to the Convocations (see paragraph 7.14).

The General Synod

(A)   MEMBERSHIP AND SIZE

13.10   We believe that too many members of the General Synod, particularly in the House of Clergy, are elected by 'special constituencies'. We have, in general, proceeded on the principle that a 'special constituency' is not justified if the relevant group can be expected to secure adequate representation through the general electoral process. Conversely a 'special constituency' is, we think, justified where a significant group would otherwise be denied representation. Our recommendations for the reduction of 'special constituencies' would effect a significant reduction in the size of the House of Clergy but would, we believe, not undermine the representative quality of the House. We believe this to be a desirable objective for reasons of both effectiveness and economy. We also propose a significant reduction in the size of the House of Laity. Our detailed recommendations are:

- that the provisions of Canon H3 and the rules made thereunder which provide for the election of six suffragan bishops to the Upper House of the Convocation of Canterbury, and three to the Upper House of the Convocation of York, be replaced by a provision that four should be elected by their peers to the House of Bishops from the Province of Canterbury and two shall be so elected from the Province of York (paragraph 8.11).

- that the Bishop of Dover be an ex-officio member of the House of Bishops and that Canon H3 be amended accordingly (see paragraph 8.12).

- that the provisions of Canon H2 and the rules made thereunder which secure 15 places in the House of Clergy for deans and provosts elected by their peers be repealed and that deans and provosts should be qualified as electors and eligible for election to the House of Clergy from their dioceses (see paragraph 8.27).

- that the deans and the residentiary canons of the Collegiate Churches of St Peter in Westminster and of St George Windsor and the Cathedral Church of Holy Trinity in Gibraltar should be qualified as electors and be eligible for election to the House of Clergy within the dioceses of London, Oxford and Gibraltar in Europe respectively (see paragraph 8.28).

- that the provisions of Canon H2 and the rules made thereunder which secure one place in the House of Clergy for either the Dean of Jersey or the Dean of Guernsey be repealed (see paragraph 8.29).

- that the provisions of Canon H2 and the rules made thereunder which secure a place in the House of Clergy for one archdeacon chosen by his peers in each diocese be repealed (see paragraph 8.33).

- that the provisions of Canon H2 which secure ex-officio places in the House of Clergy for the three senior chaplains of the armed forces should be replaced by a provision that the house of clergy of each of the three archdeaconry synods of the armed forces should elect one of their chaplains to the House of Clergy (see paragraph 8.38).

- that the provision in Canon H2 which secures an ex-officio place in the House of Clergy for the Chaplain General of

Prisons be replaced by a provision that prison chaplains (including the Chaplain General) should be eligible for election to the House of Clergy from their dioceses (see paragraph 8.40).

- that the provisions of Canon H2 and the rules made there-under which secure the election by their peers to the House of Clergy of two clerical members of religious communities, from each Province, be replaced by a provision that one member should be elected by the clerical members of communities in both Provinces (see paragraph 8.43).

- that the provisions of Canon H2 which secure six places in the House of Clergy to be elected by certain universities be repealed (see paragraph 8.46).

- that the provisions of the Church Representation Rules which secure the election by their peers to the House of Laity of the General Synod of two lay members of religious communities from the Province of Canterbury and one from the Province of York be replaced by a provision that one such member should be elected by the lay members of communities in each Province (see paragraph 8.47).

- that the Channel Islands (Representation) Measure 1931 be repealed and that, so far as necessary, Rule 36 of the Church Representation Rules be amended to provide that candidates from the deaneries of Jersey and Guernsey shall be eligible for election to the House of Laity in the same way as any other lay candidates from the diocese of Winchester (see paragraph 8.48).

- that provision be made in the Church Representation Rules that the houses of laity of each of the three archdeaconry synods of the armed forces be entitled to elect one lay person to the House of Laity (see paragraph 8.49).

- that in future the size of the General Synod should be 390 made up as shown in the table at paragraph 8.60.

- that the Archbishop of Canterbury and the Archbishop of York jointly should have power to appoint up to five members of the General Synod who may be either clerical or lay and will sit as members of the House of Clergy or the House of Laity accordingly (see paragraph 8.64).

(B)   STYLE AND PROCEDURE

13.11   It is impossible usefully to summarise the views we express in Chapter 9 of the report in which we discuss miscellaneous issues arising with respect to the style and procedure of proceedings in the General Synod. Our detailed recommendations are:

- that more imaginative use should be made of pauses for prayer and quiet reflection during meetings of the General Synod (see paragraph 9.6).

- that when a vote is to be taken, it would be more appropriate for the Legal Adviser to call upon members to 'Vote!' than to 'Divide!' (see paragraph 9.10).

- that the requirements of Article 3 (1) of the Constitution of the General Synod that it shall meet in session at least twice a year be repealed and that the Synod be free to determine the frequency of its own meetings (see paragraph 9.24).

- that when a debate on a diocesan synod motion is appropriate it should be given a measure of priority over other business (see paragraph 9.30).

- that a member of the General Synod wishing to raise an issue for debate should first be required to table the appropriate motion in his or her diocesan synod (see paragraph 9.33).

The electoral system

13.12   Our recommendations in relation to deanery synods, whose lay members at present constitute the electorate to houses of laity of diocesan synods and the House of Laity of the General Synod, would in any event require us to recommend a new basis for those elections. But even if deanery synods were to continue unchanged, we do not think that they would constitute a satisfactory electorate to the higher levels of synodical government. We have rejected the alternative of election by all persons whose names are on parish electoral rolls, primarily on the grounds that it would be very difficult to ensure that the electorate was sufficiently well informed and it is doubtful whether more than a small percentage would exercise their vote. Moreover it would be organisationally difficult and very expensive. Instead we propose that each parish should elect one or more lay persons to act as synodical electors with no other duties to perform than to vote for lay candidates in all synodical elections. We believe that such a body of electors, which would be similar in size to the laity of deanery synods, should be able both fairly to represent the views of parishes and adequately to inform themselves of the issues involved and of the qualities of the candidates standing for election. Our detailed recommendations are:

- that 10 per cent of the retired clergy in each diocese with permission to officiate be elected by their peers as electors both to the House of Clergy of the General Synod and to the house of clergy of the diocesan synod and that all retired clergy with a permission to officiate should be eligible to stand as candidates for election (see paragraph 10.3 and 10.20).

- that each parish should elect at its annual parochial church meeting a number of lay people, to be known as synodical electors, who would form the electorate for the laity in the General Synod and the diocesan synod; each parish should elect one elector for each 50 members, or part thereof, on its electoral roll (see paragraph 10.13).

- that provision should be made for the election of synodical electors by cathedral worshippers in like terms to those of Rule 27 of the Church Representation Rules which relate to the election of such worshippers to a deanery synod (paragraph 10.14).

The implications of our recommendations

13.13 Our recommendations, if accepted, will require the amendment or repeal of several Measures, Canons (and rules made under them), the Church Representation Rules and the Standing Orders of the General Synod. We recognise that this will be a substantial task in terms of resources and time. We believe, as we have said, that, once in place, the amendments we propose will significantly 'lighten the burden' and provide 'the maximum scope for exercise of local discretion consistent with having a national framework for the Church's government.' We have not found it possible fully to assess all the financial implications of our recommendations. We are confident however that once the proposed new arrangements are in place they will not give rise to additional expenditure, rather the reverse. For example, the reduction we propose in the size of the General Synod and the scope we envisage for it to limit the issues it needs to address (and the frequency of its meetings) certainly provide room for significant savings as, we believe, do our recommendations in respect of deanery synods. In reaching this view we have in mind the cost of synodical government not only in terms of finance but in terms also of the time and energy of church people, resources which may, then, perhaps be devoted to other means of furthering the Gospel.

Appendix I

The government of the Church of England: an historical note

1   The institutional structure of the Church of England, giving it the character which we recognise in describing it as the 'Established Church,' was impressed upon it after the breach with Rome in the reigns of Henry VIII and Elizabeth I. The Acts of Supremacy of 1534 and 1558 established the supremacy of the Sovereign over the Church. Successive Acts of Uniformity in 1548, 1552 and 1558 prescribed the Church's forms of worship. These outstanding landmarks in Anglican legislative history reflect the common assumption of English society in the sixteenth century that Church and State constituted a single entity which properly fell to be ruled by a single government. No doubt the personal influence of the Sovereign throughout the Tudor period was the dominant factor. But in the reign of Queen Elizabeth I the role of Parliament was no mere formality and at that time the idea of Parliament as fully competent to speak for the laity of the Church of England corresponded to reality. The idea has had a profound constitutional influence ever since.

2   The Convocations had originated under the Plantagenet kings. In the late thirteenth and early fourteenth centuries the Crown's attempts to secure the attendance in Parliament of representatives of the lower clergy with the object of obtaining their consent to taxation were successfully resisted. A compromise between the Church and the Crown led to a situation in which assemblies of bishops, abbots, priors, deans, archdeacons and representatives of the lower clergy met in response to the summons, not directly of the King, but of the Archbishops acting in response to the King's request, in order to vote subsidies to the Crown. These were the first assemblies called by the name Convocations. They were originally concerned only with fiscal matters and were distinct from the provincial or synodical councils of much earlier origin which exercised

authority over a wide range of ecclesiastical affairs and in which the lower clergy had not been regularly represented. But over the following century there was a gradual fusion of these bodies and from the fifteenth century onwards the term Convocations has been applied to the representative bodies of the clergy in the Provinces of Canterbury and York exercising the functions originally inherited from the provincial councils.

3   At the Reformation the Convocations exchanged the authority of the Pope for the authority of the Crown. Henry VIII could look for a precedent to the Emperor Justinian (in several respects the King's explicit model) who legislated in his Codes and Novels to provide the standard texts of Church Law for the sixth-century Roman Empire. By the Submission of the Clergy Act 1533 the English clergy were no longer to assemble save in response to the King's writ, their Canons were henceforth to require the Royal Assent and no Canon was to be made or enforced contrary to the Royal Prerogative or the laws of the realm. Subject to these restraints the Convocations nevertheless enjoyed and exercised a substantial degree of legislative freedom independently of Parliament in purely ecclesiastical affairs from the accession of Queen Elizabeth I until the Commonwealth. They continued also to vote subsidies to the Crown, providing a form of taxation of the clergy in respect of their benefices, until, in 1664, the clergy finally submitted to liability to general taxation by Parliament.

4   With the Restoration, following the religious and constitutional conflicts which split society in the middle years of the seventeenth century, came the Act of Uniformity 1662 which gave statutory authority to the Book of Common Prayer, as we know it, and represented the last attempt to enforce religious unity upon the whole country. Such success as it had was short lived. The Revolution of 1688 marked the end of the Sovereign's exercise of significant personal influence over Church affairs and the development of constitutional monarchy meant that the Crown's supremacy was effectively superseded by the supremacy of Parliament. The Toleration Act of 1689 was the first of a long series of statutes which, over the years, have gradually freed persons of other Christian denominations and persons professing other religions or no religion from the civil disabilities to which they were formerly subject.

5   In the last years of the seventeenth century attempts by the Convocation of Canterbury to effect what were seen as urgently needed reforms in the corpus of Canon law were largely frustrated by controversies between the Upper and Lower Houses. These controversies continued intermittently through the reigns of William and Mary and Queen Anne. In 1717 they came to a head in a dispute which induced King George I's Ministers to advise him to issue a writ requiring the prorogation of Convocation and this in turn ushered in the long period when the Convocations were totally inactive.

6   Throughout the eighteenth century and for much of the nineteenth century the only legislation enacted which affected the Church was that issuing from Parliament. Not surprisingly, considering the great changes taking place during this period in so many aspects of social life, the volume of ecclesiastical statutes enacted gradually increased from an average of less than three a year before 1760 to more than 25 a year between 1820 and 1870. At the same time the repeal of the Test and Corporation Acts in 1828 and the Roman Catholic Emancipation in 1829 strengthened the view of many that Parliament could no longer be regarded as truly representative of the laity of the Church of England. Meetings of the Convocations at this time were mere formalities, but the movement to restore to them an active role in the affairs of the Church gained ground against opposition until by the mid 1850s the Convocation of Canterbury was regularly meeting for the discussion of church business, and in the second half of the nineteenth century was an active forum for the examination of the problems confronting the Church and was able to effect some revision of the Canon law. The Convocation of York resumed an active role in 1861.

7   Much of the opposition to the revival of the Convocations had come from those who regarded them as unrepresentative and thought that reform of their constitution should precede any resumption of activity. But beyond this there was a growing body of opinion that the laity should be directly involved in the government of the Church. Voluntary movements in the second half of the nineteenth century led to the setting up of parochial church councils and ruridecanal and diocesan conferences as informal bodies in which the laity could at least play some part in the direction of Church affairs. In 1884 it was proposed that Houses of Laymen should meet at the

same time as the Convocations. The Canterbury House of Laymen first met in 1886, the York House of Laymen in 1892 and in 1898 provision was made for the two provincial Houses of Laymen to meet jointly. Their primary function was advisory, particularly in relation to matters requiring parliamentary legislation.

8   In 1898 Archbishop Frederick Temple appointed a Joint Committee of the Canterbury Convocation to examine the position of the laity in the Church. The Committee reported in 1902.[1] Their report contains a comprehensive and scholarly historical study of the part played by the laity in the government of the Church from the earliest times. In expressing their conclusions the members of the Committee write:

> 'The study of the Apostolic and primitive constitution of the Church, as it is set forth in Holy Scripture and in the history and writings of the first three centuries, shows, as we think, clearly the co-ordinate action of clergy and laity as integral parts of the whole body of Christ. . . . We find, in fact, in this first period traces of the co-operation of clergy and laity in all the three spheres with which our Report is concerned, in legislative functions, in the election of Church officers, and in judicial discipline, and we cannot but conclude that this co-operation belongs to the true ideal of the Church.'

9   Later, after referring to the changes in English society since the Toleration Act 1689 to which the report had devoted an earlier chapter, they write that a survey of these changes

> 'forces us to the conclusion that our laymen have lost the constitutional authority they once had in Church legislation as well as in most other parts of ecclesiastical administration. In this way also the very important conception that a layman is a member of the Church, under the discipline of the body, who has responsibilities as well as rights, has been much obscured.'

---

1   *The Position of the Laity in the Church, being the Report of the Joint Committee of the Convocation of Canterbury* (1902), Church Information Board, reprinted 1952.

The formal resolution of the Committee expressed the desirability of the formation of a National Council 'fully representing the clergy and laity of the Church of England' and envisaged that the constitution of the Council should be determined by the two Convocations meeting jointly with the Provincial Houses of Laymen 'with a view to its receiving statutory authority.'

10   There seems no reason to doubt that the 1902 Report of the Joint Committee has exercised a continuing influence on later developments in the Church of England throughout this century. But its only immediate consequence was the establishment in 1903 of a Representative Church Council which nevertheless remained a purely deliberative body with no statutory powers.

11   In 1913, at the request of the Representative Church Council, the Archbishops appointed a committee under the chairmanship of the Earl of Selborne with terms of reference 'to inquire what changes are advisable in order to secure in the relations of Church and State a fuller expression of the spiritual independence of the Church as well as of the national recognition of religion.' Their voluminous Report[2] was presented in 1916. The committee included three bishops, three lay peers and six members of the House of Commons. They concluded that 'the constitution of Parliament prevents its being in any true sense representative of the Church, and the experience of recent years has shown that it possesses neither time nor inclination nor knowledge for dealing with ecclesiastical affairs.' The committee recommended 'the formation of a Church Council which shall have power to legislate on ecclesiastical affairs subject to constitutional safeguards.' The detailed recommendations of the committee provided, in substance, the model for the National Assembly of the Church of England whose constitution was set out in an Appendix to the Address presented to His Majesty by the Convocations of Canterbury and York in May 1919.

12   The Church Assembly comprised the three Houses of Bishops, Clergy and Laity. The House of Bishops consisted of the members of the Upper Houses, and the House of Clergy consisted of the members of the Lower Houses, of the Convocations of Canterbury and York. The rules for the representation of the laity provided for parish electoral rolls based on a baptismal qualification with parish

---

2   *The Archbishops' Committee on Church and State*, SPCK, 1916.

electors electing members of ruridecanal conferences. The House of Laity of the Church Assembly consisted of representatives elected every five years by members of diocesan conferences.

13   Motions in the Church Assembly, in order to pass, required the assent of a majority present and voting in each House. The functions of the Assembly were widely defined but subject to the following significant restrictions:

(i)   'Any measure touching doctrinal formulae or the services or ceremonies of the Church of England or the administration of the Sacraments or sacred rites thereof' was to be debated and voted upon by each of the three Houses sitting separately and was to be accepted or rejected by the Assembly in the terms in which it was finally proposed by the House of Bishops.

(ii)   The Assembly was not to 'issue any statement purporting to define the doctrine of the Church of England on any question of theology.'

(iii) Nothing in the Constitution was to be 'deemed to diminish or derogate from any of the powers belonging to the Convocations . . . or of any House thereof.'

14   The Church of England Assembly (Powers) Act 1919 (the 1919 Act) provided a procedure for Measures passed by the Church Assembly to acquire the force of statute. Since the Act continues in force unamended (save in so far as it now applies to Measures passed by the General Synod in the same way as it formerly applied to Measures passed by the Church Assembly), it is convenient, when referring to the provisions of the Act, to use the present tense. A Measure which has been passed is first to be submitted to the Ecclesiastical Committee of both Houses of Parliament consisting of 15 members of the House of Lords nominated by the Lord Chancellor and 15 members of the House of Commons nominated by the Speaker. The Ecclesiastical Committee is to make a report 'stating the nature and legal effect of the Measure and its views as to the expediency thereof, especially with relation to the constitutional rights of all Her Majesty's subjects.' The report is first communicated in draft to the Legislative Committee of the General Synod and becomes a definitive report only if and when the Legislative Committee decides to present the Measure, together with the report,

to Parliament for approval. If each House of Parliament then passes a resolution directing that the Measure be presented to Her Majesty, the Measure, on receiving the Royal Assent, has the force and effect of an Act of Parliament. It is to be noted that Parliament has no power of amendment; it can only approve or reject a Measure in the form in which it was laid before Parliament by the General Synod.

15   One of the first legislative acts of the Church Assembly was to pass the Convocations of the Clergy Measure 1920 which was duly approved by both Houses of Parliament. The Measure gave power to each of the Provincial Convocations to amend by Canon the constitution of its own Lower House, and the amendments which were effected in exercise of this power secured for the first time that each Lower House should have a majority of elected over ex-officio members.

16   The effect of the restrictions on the functions of the Church Assembly to which reference has been made in paragraph 13 was to impose limitations on the role of the laity in church government which had not perhaps been anticipated. In particular, the constitution of the Assembly gave the laity no entitlement to share in the work of Canon making which remained the exclusive province of the Convocations. When a major revision of the Canon law was undertaken in the years following the Second World War, it was recognised that the laity ought to be consulted and in 1947 the Convocations resolved that Canons which had received their general approval should be submitted to the House of Laity of the Church Assembly for comment before receiving final approval. In the event this was felt to be an unsatisfactory compromise in that the laity's involvement only in the final stages of the total process denied them any significant influence on its outcome.

17   In 1953, at the request of the Church Assembly, a commission under the chairmanship of the Dean of Christ Church (the Lowe Commission) was appointed by the Archbishops 'to consider how the clergy and the laity can be joined in the synodical government of the Church.' Their report[3] paid tribute to the 'strong and learned Committee' which had produced the 1902 report[4] and endorsed their

---

3   *The Convocations and the Laity*, C.A. 1240, Church Information Board, 1958.

4   *The Position of the Laity in the Church, being the Report of the Joint Committee of the Convocation of Canterbury* (1902), Church Information Board, reprinted 1952.

conclusions to the effect 'that theology justifies, and history demonstrates, a co-ordinate action of clergy and laity as integral parts of the whole Body of Christ; that the ultimate authority and right of collective action lie with the whole Body, the Church; and that the co-operation of clergy and laity in Church government belongs to the true ideal of the Church.' The Commission's proposal to attain the realisation of this ideal was to create a new House of Laity in each of the Convocations with powers similar to those of the Lower Houses of the Clergy.

18   Although the principle of enhanced lay participation in church government was generally endorsed, the detailed proposals of the Lowe Commission were not. There followed a somewhat protracted period of debates in the Church Assembly and in the Upper and Lower Houses of both Convocations in the course of which various schemes designed to give effect to the agreed general principle were discussed, but no consensus was reached. Eventually a commission under the chairmanship of Lord Hodson (the Hodson Commission) was appointed by the Archbishops in 1964 on the basis of a compromise the emergence of which is the subject of a full account in the Report[5] which they delivered in 1966. The draft Measure recommended by the Hodson Commission was, in substance, adopted by the Church Assembly and approved by Parliament and became the Synodical Government Measure 1969. The great change, which the Measure effected by authorising the necessary legislation by Canon, was the vesting of the functions of the Convocations, with certain limited exceptions, in the Church Assembly, now renamed and reconstituted as the General Synod.

19   The Constitution of the General Synod is set out in Schedule 2 of the 1969 Measure. The constitution of the Houses of Bishops and Clergy remains as before. The House of Laity is elected in accordance with the new Church Representation Rules. As in the Church Assembly, a majority of the members of each House present and voting is generally required for the approval of any Measure or Canon. The restriction which applied to the Church Assembly, as described in paragraph 13 (i) above, is in effect retained by Article 7 of Schedule 2, in that any provision of the kind described may only be

---

5   *Synodical Government in the Church of England,* Church Information Office, 1966.

approved in the terms proposed by the House of Bishops and, in addition, the House of Laity and each House of both Convocations has an effective veto over any such provision.

20   Article 8 of Schedule 2 imposes special procedural requirements with respect to (i) any Measure or Canon providing for permanent changes in the Services of Baptism or Holy Communion or in the Ordinal, or (ii) a scheme for a constitutional union or a permanent substantial change of relationship between the Church of England and another Christian body. In either case, before the Measure, Canon or scheme may be approved by the General Synod, it must be approved by a majority of the dioceses at meetings of their diocesan synods. In the first case approval by the General Synod requires a majority of not less than two-thirds of those present and voting in each House. In the second case the General Synod itself may provide by resolution that the final approval of the scheme shall require the assent of special majorities as specified in the resolution.

21   The 1969 Measure established diocesan and deanery synods and prescribed their statutory functions. It also provided, by the Church Representation Rules set out in Schedule 3, a complete electoral system. Members of parochial church councils are elected by the persons on the electoral roll of the parish who also elect members of the house of laity of their deanery synod. Members of the house of laity of each deanery synod elect members to the house of laity of their diocesan synod and also to the House of Laity of the General Synod.

22   Since the Church Assembly was given legislative power by the 1919 Act, the only occasions of major significance when attempts to exercise that power were frustrated were in 1927 and 1928 when the Measure authorising the use of the revised Prayer Book as an alternative to the Prayer Book of 1662 was rejected by the House of Commons. The inability of the Church to regulate its own forms of worship remained a potential source of conflict until 1965 when, by approving the Prayer Book (Alternative and Other Services) Measure, Parliament enabled the Church lawfully to introduce new forms of service on an experimental basis and for a temporary period. In the following year, however, the Archbishops appointed a Commission under the chairmanship of the Reverend Professor Owen Chadwick

(the Chadwick Commission) with terms of reference 'to make recommendations as to the modifications in the constitutional
relationship between Church and State which are desirable and practicable and in so doing to take account of current and future steps to
promote greater unity between Churches.' The deliberations of this
body overlapped with those of the Hodson Commission, and their
report did not appear until 1970.[6]

23   It was this report which led in due course to the enactment of
the Church of England (Worship and Doctrine) Measure 1974, the
last and perhaps the most significant of the statutory reforms to
shape and determine the powers of the Church's own legislative body
as they are today. Under the 1974 Measure it lies with the General
Synod, without the need to resort to Parliament, to make provision
by Canon (i) 'with respect to worship in the Church of England,
including provision for empowering the General Synod to approve,
amend, continue or discontinue forms of service,' and (ii) 'with
respect to the obligations of the clergy, deaconesses and lay officers
of the Church of England to assent or subscribe to the doctrine of
that Church.' A Canon made in exercise of either power requires the
final approval of a two-thirds majority of those present and voting in
each House and every Canon is to be 'such as in the opinion of the
General Synod is neither contrary to, nor indicative of any departure
from, the doctrine of the Church of England in any essential matter.'
Moreover, with respect to forms of service, the power of the General
Synod is to be so exercised 'as to ensure that the forms of service contained in the Book of Common Prayer continue to be available for
use in the Church of England.' The decision as to which forms of service authorised or approved under Canon are to be used in any parish
church is to be taken jointly by the incumbent and the parochial
church council. In case of disagreement the forms of service used are
to be those contained in the Book of Common Prayer. It is interesting to note that it was not until the passage of the 1974 Measure that
so much as remained on the statute book of the Acts of Uniformity
of 1548 and 1558 was finally repealed.

---

6   *Church and State, Report of the Archbishop's Commission*, 1970; reprinted by Church
Information Office, 1985.

Appendix II

Terms of reference, meetings, and evidence received

1   We were appointed by the Standing Committee of the General Synod in April 1993 with the following terms of reference:

> To review the system of synodical government in the Church of England introduced in 1970, with particular reference to:
>
> (i)   its rationale and effectiveness, both locally and nationally;
>
> (ii)   the composition of synods and the system of election to them;
>
> (iii)   the way synodical government operates, including its style and procedure;
>
> (iv)   communications between the different levels and with Parliament;
>
> and to make recommendations.

2   In October 1990, in preparation for our work, the Standing Committee had issued a Discussion Paper.[1] The Discussion Paper listed a series of questions which were 'thought likely to form the hard core of those which should be considered by the proposed Synodical Government Review Commission.' These were 'designed to stimulate discussion and reflection in the church at diocesan, deanery and parochial level, on the questions to which the Review Commission, when appointed, will have to address itself.' The Revd Andrew Baughen very kindly prepared for us a detailed analysis of the responses made to this Discussion Paper and we are grateful to him for his work.

---

1   *Synodical Government 1970–1990: The First Twenty Years'*, GS Misc 344, Church House Publishing, 1990.

3   In September 1993, we invited further comments and suggestions from individuals or groups through a letter in the Church and National Press. We also invited comments and suggestions from members of the General Synod. Attached is a list of those individuals, institutions and organisations who wrote to us; we are grateful to each of them for writing.

4   At our invitation the Bishop of Chichester, author of the Bampton Lectures for 1960,[2] came to one of our meetings, as did the Bishop of Ballarat (Rt Revd David Silk, then Prolocutor of the Lower House of the Convocation of Canterbury, and Archdeacon of Leicester). We also met with members of the Faith and Order Advisory Group of the Council for Christian Unity.

5   We decided at an early stage in our work that it would be important to seek to arrange to visit a number of dioceses in order to hear directly about the experience and concerns of those in dioceses about the operation of synodical government. With the very willing co-operation of the dioceses concerned we were able to arrange 24-hour visits to the dioceses of Birmingham, Chelmsford, Liverpool, London, Portsmouth, Salisbury and York in May and June 1995. In the course of those visits members of the Group met in nearly all cases with the bishops, the suffragan or area bishops, the chairmen of the DBF, the dean or provost, the diocesan secretaries, the archdeacons, the clerical and the lay chairmen of the diocesan synod, rural deans and lay chairmen of deanery synods, members of the bishop's council, and other clergy and lay people interested in, but not actively involved with, synodical government identified by the dioceses themselves. These visits proved enormously valuable to us as we considered the recommendations we should make. We are grateful for the time and hospitality that all those concerned so readily offered us.

6   In the course of our work since 1993 we have met together on 19 occasions for meetings for the most part of a day and on three occasions residentially over a period of 24 hours.

---

2   *Council and Consent – Aspects of the Government of the Church as exemplified in the History of the English Provincial Synods*, SPCK, 1961.

Individuals who submitted evidence

The Revd C. Abbott

The Revd M. Adams

The Revd H. Allen & Mr Sunderland

Canon D. Ambrose

The Revd & Mrs A. H. Apps

Mr W. J. K. Arnold

Mr J. H. Arrowsmith-Brown

Rt Revd John Austin, Bishop of Aston

Mr T. Aves

Mr M. Ayles

Mrs C. E. Baines

Mr D. Baker

Mr S. G. Baker

Mrs J. Bale

Mr E. Bardsley

The Revd Edwin Barnes

Mr/Mrs H. W. Barnes

Mr Jim Baverstock

P. G. Bazeley

Lt Cdr N. R. Beach

Mr L. W. Bean

Mrs W. L. Becker

Mr D. Beckwith

The Revd A. F. Bell

Mr A. Bending

The Revd E. J. Bewes

Dr E. G. W. Bill

Canon G. N. Bird

Pamela Bishop

The Revd P. L. Bishop

The Revd Bryan Blyth

Barbara Bourne

Mr Bowen

Miss A. S. Bowyer-Bower

Mrs E. V. Braqq

Mrs J. Brearley

Canon J. H. Brewer

The Revd Bob Britton

The Revd D. Bubbers

Bp Colin Buchanan

Mr Brian Bull & Dr Barbara Judge

Mr J. R. Burgan

Mr A. Burnand

Judge Bursell

The Revd D. Butterfield

Ven B. A. C. Kirk-Duncan

Mr/Mrs P. C. Warren

Mr W. J. C. Caley

Miss E. M. Cannon

Mr H. Capstick

N. D. J. Carne

Canon C. T. Catton

Mr M. A. Catty

Mr P. G. Cavalier

Mr V. Chalcraft

Mr D. Chalk

Mrs E. F. Chapman

Mr G. Charrington

Miss A. Chater

The Revd J. de Chazel

Rt Revd Michael Baughen, Bishop of Chester

The Revd L. J. Chesterman

Mr W. S. Chilcraft

Mrs S. M. Clayton

Dr A. C. Clifford

Colonel C. G. Clymow

Sir James Cobban

The Revd B. W. Coleman

The Revd Flt Lt I. R. Colson

Ms B. Cooke

Mr D. Cooper

Mr Hugh Craig

Mr F. Cranmer

Canon R. C. Craston

Colonel J. H. G. Crompton

Mr Cresswell

Mr J. P. Cryer

Mr D. Cubitt

The Revd R. D. Payne

Mr/Mrs D. Jordan

The Revd R. Daniel

Mr A. Davidson

Mr Robin Davies

Mrs I. Didan

Mr G. J. Dignum

Mr/Mrs A. Dobbs

Mr K. Dodgson

Canon M. Doe

Ms Hazel Door

Mr R. F. Dorey

Mr A. G. Douglas

The Revd G. Francis Dow

Mr J. Ellis

Mr H. W. Ellis

Sheila Evans (4 letters)

The Rt Revd David Evans

Mr S. F. Every

The Revd J. A. Exall

Mr A. M. Fagg

Mr W. Featherstone

The Revd Alan Fell

The Revd D. W. Finch

The Revd D. C. Flatt

Mrs Meyrich Flemington

Mr R. E. Ford

The Revd P. Forster

The Revd T. R. Fowke

Mr W. E. Furness

Mr Garrud
Mr J. Geller
Dr P. Giddings
Mrs P. Giordani
Mr E. Gittings
The Revd D. Gooderham
Louise Graham
Canon G. T. Gray
Miss A. Green
Mr A. T. Gregory
Mr R. M. Hall
Mr J. I. Harbidge
Mrs M. E. Harris
The Revd D. M. Hartley
Mr F. D. Hemingway
Mr C. E. Herbert
Mr R. J. Herd
The Revd J. K. Hewitt
The Revd P. M. Hickley
Mr D. Hillman
Mr C. Hinton
Mr Francis Howcutt
Mrs M. M. Hubrer
Canon K. Hugo
Mr J. P. Humphery
Mr D. A. Hunter
  Johnston
The Revd John Huntriss
Capt J. Hurworth RN
Mrs A. E. Hutchins
Miss G. M. Jackson
Mr T. D. R. James
Mr T. Jenkins
Canon Jenkins
Mr D. Jones
Mr D. Jordan
Mr M. F. Keef
Mr P. R. Kinderman
The Archdeacon of
  Lancaster
The Revd H. R. Lau
The Revd P. Lee

Mr A. Leeding
Miss B. H. Lepper
The Revd M. Lesiter
Miss D. Lethbridge
Rt Revd Ian Cundy,
  Bishop of Lewes
Archdeacon of Lewes
  and Hastings
Mr J. J. G. Lewis
The Revd D. Lickess
The Revd F. H. Linn
Mrs J. Loveless
Sir Douglas Lovelock
The Revd M. Malsom
Mr G. Mann
Miss J. C. Mann
Mr J. Marks
Mr R. F. Marriott
Major H. E. R. Martin
Col P. Massey
The Revd P. D. May
Mr Brian McHenry (3
  letters)
Professor D. McClean
Colonel R. R. McNish
Miss E. Miller
Mr R. Mills
Mr M. H. D. Milne
Mr J. I. Mitchell
Mr B. Morgan
Mr B. S. Morris
Mr A. C. F. Mortimer
The Revd A. J. Mortimer
Mr L. Mutum
Air Commodore Nance
Mr P. W. Nelson
Mrs G. F. Newton
The Revd J. C. S. Nias
Mr J. U. Nichol
Mrs A. Nichols
Mr F. R. North
Mr N. R. Nottidge

Mrs H. D. O'Sullivan
Miss A. Ottley
Mr H. Owen
Mr R. Pain
Mrs E. Palamountain
Mr R. R. Panter (2 let-
  ters)
Mr N. D. Parker
The Revd G. H. Paton
The Revd J. Paul
Mr P. T. Pearce
Mr C. R. Pendry
Mr D. Pennant
Mrs E. Perry
Rt Revd William
  Westwood, Bishop of
  Peterborough
Mrs P. D. Peterken
Miss P. Phillimore
Mr Phythian
Mrs N. Pickthall
Prof. Pollard
Mr T. M. Powell
Mrs Penelope Puntis
Mr Roy Pybus
Mr B. J. Pyke
Mr R. Radford
Mr M. J. Rambridge
Mr D. Ramsell
Rene Read
The Revd D. S. R.
  Redman
Mrs J. M. P. Reid
The Revd Robert Reiss
Mr D. Riding
Mr H. Ridout
Mrs B. Ritchie
Cdr A. D. Roake
Mr H. Roberts
Mr Peter Robottom
Mr Frank Robson
The Revd A. L. Rose

Mr L. W. Rowan

The Archdeacon of Salop

Mr P. Scarlett

The Preb R. Schofield

Mr M. Scott

The Revd K. Scott

Mr R. Scott

Mr P. J. Searby

The Revd T. R. Selwyn-Smith

Mr Michael Shaw

Mr H. Shaw

Mr A. T. R. Shelley

The Revd R. A. Shone

David Simpson

Mr M. Sinden

The Revd Chris Skilton

Mr E. H. Skinner

Mr J. Smallwood

Mrs D. Smith

Mrs M. Smyth

The Revd R. Speck

Mr Nigel Speller (2 letters)

Mr A. R. Spencer

Mr A. T. Stafford

Mr H. W. G. Stamper

Mr T. Stevenson

Mr L. Stretch

Mr J. Sudbury

Miss M. N. Swift

Mr T. Swinnerton

Major P. G. Tanner

Mr P. Thomas

Mrs A. C. B. Toms (2 letters)

The Revd Dr H. Turner

Mr D. A. Tyrrell

Mr P. R. Unwin

Mrs F. O. Urwin

Miss N. Vincent

M. Wakham

Col R. L. Wallis

Mr J. H. E. Watson

Mr E. V. Weekes

Miss A. A. M. Wells

Mr Jim White (2 letters)

Dr M. White

Mr N. W. Whitton

Mrs C. Williams

Mrs Shirley-Ann Williams

Capt D. Williamson RN

Mr R. Williamson

Mr P. L. Windsor

Colonel M. J. World

Mr A. R. D. Wright

Miss D. V. S. Wright

Mr P. W. Wright

Dr J. Yallop

The Revd J. K. Young

Miss J. Young

Organisations and institutions which submitted evidence

Anglican Voluntary Societies Forum

Church House Deaneries Group

The Church's Ministry among the Jews

The Church Society

The Church Union

Churches Together in England

Deaneries:

Derwent	(Diocese of York)
Midsomer Norton	(Diocese of Bath & Wells)
Redbridge	(Diocese of Chelmsford)

Dioceses:

Birmingham	Exeter	Norwich	Salisbury
Blackburn	Guildford	Oxford	Sheffield
Bradford	Hereford	Peterborough	Sodor & Man
Chelmsford	Leicester	Portsmouth	Southwark
Coventry	Lichfield	Ripon	Truro
Derby	Lincoln	Rochester	Winchester
Durham	Liverpool	St Albans	York
Ely	London	St Edmundsbury & Ipswich	

Forces Synodical Council

The English Clergy Association

General Synod of the Church of England:

> House of Bishops
> House of Clergy
> House of Laity
> Committee for Minority Ethnic Anglican Concerns
> Dioceses Commission
> Partnership for World Mission

Mothers' Union

Parishes:

Aveton Gifford	(Diocese of Exeter)
Hellingly & Upper Dicker	(Diocese of Chichester)
Westleigh	(Diocese of Exeter)

Retired Clergy Association

Appendix III

Legislative and other references

1. Church electoral roll

Rule 1 of the Church Representation Rules provide:

'(1)   There shall be a church electoral roll (in these rules referred to as 'the roll') in every parish, on which the names of lay persons shall be entered as hereinafter provided. The roll shall be available for inspection by bona fide inquirers.

(2)   A lay person shall be entitled to have his name entered on the roll of a parish if he is baptised, of sixteen years or upwards, has signed an application form for enrolment set out in Appendix I of these rules and declares himself either –

(a)   to be a member of the Church of England or of a Church in communion therewith resident in the parish; or

(b)   to be such a member and, not being resident in the parish, to have habitually attended public worship in the parish during a period of six months prior to enrolment; or

(c)   to be a member in good standing of a Church which subscribes to the doctrine of the Holy Trinity (not being a Church in communion with the Church of England) and also prepared to declare himself to be a member of the Church of England having habitually attended public worship in the parish during a period of six months prior to enrolment.

Provided that where a lay person will have his sixteenth birthday after the intended revision of the electoral roll or the preparation of a new roll but on or before the date of the annual parochial church meeting, he may complete a form of application for enrolment and his name shall be enrolled but with effect from the date of his birthday.

(3)   Where a person resides in an extra-parochial place he shall be deemed for the purposes of these rules to reside in the parish which it abuts, and if there is any doubt in the matter a determination shall be made by the bishop's council and standing committee.

(4)   A person shall be entitled to have his name on the roll of each of any number of parishes if he is entitled by virtue of paragraphs (2) and (3) of this rule to have his name entered on each roll; but a person whose name is entered on the roll of each of two or more parishes must choose one of those parishes for the purpose of the provisions of these rules which prescribe the qualifications for election to a deanery synod, a diocesan synod or the General Synod or for membership of a parochial church council under rule 14 (1) (f) or of a deanery synod under rule 24 (6) (b).

(5)   The roll shall, until a parochial church council has been constituted in a parish be formed and revised by the minister and churchwardens (if any), and shall, after such council has been constituted, be kept and revised by or under the direction of the council. Reference in this rule to a parochial church council shall, so far as may be necessary for giving effect to these rules, be construed as including references to the minister and churchwardens (if any).

(6)   Where a new parish is created by a pastoral scheme, the roll of that parish shall in the first instance consist –

    (a)   in the case of a parish created by the union of two or more former parishes, of the rolls of those parishes combined to form one roll;

    (b)   by any other case, of the names of the persons whose names are at the date of the coming into existence of the new parish entered on the roll of a parish the whole or any part of which forms part of the new parish and who are either resident in the new parish or have habitually attended public worship therein.

(7) The parochial church council shall appoint a church electoral roll officer to act under its direction for the purpose of carrying out its functions with regard to the electoral roll.

(8) The names of persons who are entitled to have their names entered upon the roll of a parish shall, subject to the provisions of these rules, be from time to time added to the roll. It shall be the duty of the electoral roll officer to keep the roll constantly up to date by the addition and removal of names as from time to time required by these rules and to report such additions and removals at the next meeting of the parochial church council.

(9) Subject to the provision of this rule, a person's name shall, as the occasion arises, be removed from the roll, if he –

(a) has died; or

(b) becomes a clerk in Holy Orders; or

(c) signifies in writing his desire that his name should be removed; or

(d) ceases to reside in the parish, unless after so ceasing he continues, in any period of six months, habitually to attend public worship in the parish, unless prevented from doing so by illnesses or other sufficient cause; or

(e) is not resident in the parish and has not habitually attended public worship in the parish during the preceding six months, not having been prevented from doing so by illness or other sufficient cause; or

(f) was not entitled to have his name entered on the roll at the time when it was entered.

(10) The removal of a person's name from the roll under any of the provisions of these rules shall be without prejudice to his right to have his name entered again, if he has or acquires that right.

(11) The roll shall where practicable contain a record of the address of every person whose name is entered on the roll, but a failure to comply with this requirement shall not prejudice the validity of any entry on the roll.'

Appendix III.2

2. Membership of the PCC

Rule 14 (1) of the Church Representation Rules provides that membership of the PCC shall consist of:

'(a) all clerks in Holy Orders beneficed in or licensed to the parish;

(b) any deaconess or lay worker licensed to the parish;

(c) in the case of a parish in the area of a benefice for which a team ministry is established, all the members of the team of that ministry;

(d) the churchwardens, being actual communicants whose names are on the roll of the parish;

(e) such, if any, of the readers who are licensed to that parish or licensed to an area which includes that parish and whose names are on the roll of the parish as the annual meeting may determine;

(f) all persons whose names are on the roll of the parish and who are lay members of any deanery synod, diocesan synod or the General Synod;

(g) such number of representatives of the laity as the annual meeting may decide, and so that the number determined may be altered from time to time by a resolution passed at any annual meeting, but such resolution shall not take effect before the next ensuing annual meeting; and

(h) co-opted members, if the parochial church council so decides, not exceeding in number one-fifth of the representatives of the laity elected under the last preceding sub-paragraph of this paragraph or two persons whichever shall be the greater, and being either clerks in Holy Orders or actual lay communicants of sixteen years of age or upwards. The term of office of a co-opted member shall be until the conclusion of the next annual meeting; but without prejudice to his being co-opted on subsequent occasions for a similar term, subject to and in accordance with the provisions of these rules.'

Appendix III.3

3. Functions of PCCs

Section 2 of the Parochial Church Councils (Powers) Measure 1956 (as amended by section 6 of the Synodical Government Measure 1969) provides:

'(1) It shall be the duty of the incumbent and the parochial church council to consult together on matters of general concern and importance to the parish.

(2) The functions of parochial church councils shall include –

    (a) co-operation with the incumbent in promoting in the parish the whole mission of the Church, pastoral, evangelistic, social and ecumenical;

    (b) the consideration and discussion of matters concerning the Church of England or any other matters of religious or public interest, but not the declaration of the doctrine of the Church on any question;

    (c) making known and putting into effect any provision made by the diocesan synod or the deanery synod, but without prejudice to the powers of the council on any particular matter;

    (d) giving advice to the diocesan synod and the deanery synod on any matter referred to the council;

    (e) raising such matters as the council consider appropriate with the diocesan synod or deanery synod.

(3) In the exercise of its functions the parochial church council shall take into consideration any expression of opinion by any parochial church meeting.'

Appendix III.4

4. The Chairman of the PCC

The following provisions are made in Appendix II of the Church Representation Rules concerning the chairman of the PCC:

'Power to Call Meetings

3   The chairman may at any time convene a meeting of the council. If he refuses or neglects to do so within seven days after a requisition for that purpose signed by not less than one-third of the members of the council has been presented to him those members may forthwith convene a meeting.'

'Chairman at Meetings

5   Subject to the provisions of rules 22 and 23 the chair at a meeting of the council shall be taken –

    (a)   by the chairman of the council if he is present;

    (b)   subject to paragraphs (c) and (d) hereof, if the chairman of the council is not present, by the vice-chairman of the council if he is present;

    (c)   if the benefice is vacant and a minister acting as priest-in-charge of a parish in respect of which rights of presentation are suspended, by the priest-in-charge;

    (d)   in the case of a parish in the area of a benefice for which a team ministry is established, by the rector in that ministry if he is present and both the vicar in that ministry who would if he were present be entitled, by virtue of a provision in a pastoral scheme or the bishop's licence, to preside and the vice-chairman of the council are not present:

Provided that at any such meeting the chairman presiding shall, if he thinks it expedient to do so or the meeting so resolves, vacate the chair either generally or for the purpose of any business in which he has a personal interest or for any other particular business.

Should neither the chairman, the vice-chairman nor, where sub-paragraphs (c) and (d) above apply, the priest-in-charge or rector be available to take the chair for any meeting or for any particular item on the agenda during a meeting then a chairman shall be chosen by those members present from among their number and the person so chosen shall preside for that meeting or for that particular item.'

'Short Notice for Emergency Meetings

8   In the case of sudden emergency or other special circum-stances requiring immediate action by the council a meeting may be convened by the chairman of the council at not less than three clear days' notice in writing to the members of the council but the quorum for the transaction of any business at such meetings shall be a major-ity of the then existing members of the council and no business shall be transacted at such meeting except as is specified in the notice con-vening the meeting.'

'Casting Vote

11   In the case of an equal division of votes the chairman of the meeting shall have a second or casting vote.'

Appendix III.5

5. Functions of deanery synods

Deanery Synods were created by the Synodical Government Measure 1969 with functions defined by section 5 of the Measure as follows:

'(3) The functions of a deanery synod shall be –

(a) to consider matters concerning the Church of England and to make provision for such matters in relation to their deanery, and to consider and express their opinion on any other matters of religious or public interest;

(b) to bring together the views of the parishes of the deanery on common problems, to discuss and formulate common policies on those problems, to foster a sense of community and interdependence among those parishes, and generally to promote in the deanery the whole mission of the Church, pastoral, evangelistic, social and ecumenical;

(c) to make known and so far as appropriate put into effect any provision made by the diocesan synod;

(d) to consider the business of the diocesan synod, and particularly any matters referred to that synod by the General Synod, and to sound parochial opinion whenever they are required or consider it appropriate to do so;

(e) to raise such matters as the deanery synod consider appropriate with the diocesan synod:

Provided that the functions referred to in paragraph (a) hereof shall not include the issue of any statement purporting to declare the doctrine of the Church on any question.

(4) If the diocesan synod delegate to deanery synods functions in relation to parishes of their deaneries, and in particular the determination of parochial shares in quotas allocated to the deaneries, the deanery synod shall exercise those functions.

In this subsection "quota" means an amount to be subscribed to the expenditure authorised by diocesan synods.

(5)   The General Synod may by Canon or Regulations extend, amend or further define the functions of deanery synods.'

Appendix III.6

6. Membership of deanery synods

1   The Church Representation Rules (Rule 24), provide that a deanery synod shall consist of a house of clergy and a house of laity.

Under Rule 24 (2) the house of clergy shall consist of:

'(a)   the clerks in Holy Orders beneficed in or licensed to any parish in the deanery;

(b)   any clerks in Holy Orders licensed to institutions in the deanery under the Extra-Parochial Ministry Measure 1967;

(c)   any clerical members of the General Synod or diocesan synod resident in the deanery;

(d)   such other clerks in Holy Orders holding the bishop's licence to work throughout the diocese or in more than one deanery and resident in the deanery subject to any direction which may be given by the members of the House of Clergy of the bishop's council that, having regard to the number of parochial and non-parochial clergy in the deanery, such clerk shall have membership of a specified deanery synod other than the deanery where he resides provided that no person shall thereby be a member of more than one deanery synod in the diocese;

(e)   one or more retired clerks in Holy Orders who are in receipt of a pension in accordance with the provisions of the Clergy Pensions Measure 1961 at the relevant date. One clerk may be elected or chosen for every ten retired clerks or part thereof, elected or chosen in such manner as may be approved by the bishop by and from the retired clerks who are in receipt of such a pension, are resident in the deanery and do not hold the licence of the bishop.'

2   The house of laity is prescribed by Rule 24 (6) as follows:

'(a)   the parochial representatives elected to the synod by the annual meetings of the parishes of the deanery;

(b)   any lay members of the General Synod, a diocesan synod or an area synod constituted in accordance with section 17 of the Dioceses Measure 1978 whose names are entered on the roll of any parish in the deanery;

(c)   if in the opinion of the bishop of the diocese any community of persons in the deanery who are in the spiritual care of a chaplain licensed by the bishop should be represented in that house, one lay person, being an actual communicant member of the Church of England of eighteen years or upwards, chosen in such manner as may be approved by the bishop by and from among the members of that community;

(d)   the deaconesses and lay workers licensed by the bishop to work in any part of the deanery;

(e)   such other deaconesses or lay workers holding the bishop's licence to work throughout the diocese or in more than one deanery and resident in the deanery subject to any direction which may be given by the members of the House of Laity of the bishop's council that, having regard to the number of deaconesses or lay workers in the deanery, such person shall have membership of a specified deanery synod other than the deanery where they reside provided that no person shall thereby be a member of more than one deanery synod in the diocese.'

3   The number of lay representatives elected from the parishes is determined by resolution of the diocesan synod and must be 'related to the numbers of names on the rolls of parishes . . . provided that such a resolution shall not make it possible for a parish with fewer than twenty-six names on the roll to have more than one representative.' Such lay representatives are to be elected by annual meetings every three years and hold office for a period of three years.

4   Both houses have the power (Rule 24 (7)) to co-opt additional members 'provided that the number of members co-opted by either

house shall not exceed five per cent of the total number of members of that house or three, whichever is the greater.'

5   The size of any deanery synod in the diocese 'shall not be more than 150 and, so far as is practicable, shall not be less than 50: Provided that the maximum number of 150 may be exceeded for the purpose of securing that the house of laity is not less in number than the house of clergy.' (Rule 256)

6   There is further power, under Rule 26, for the diocesan synod to make a scheme to vary Rules 24 and 25 'if it appears to the diocesan synod that the preceding rules in this part relating to the membership of deanery synods ought to be varied to meet the special circumstances of the diocese or the deaneries.' The diocesan synod may also, under Rule 27, provide for the representation on a deanery synod of the dean, provost, the residentiary canons or other ministers of the cathedral and of lay persons who are on the electoral roll of a parish church cathedral, or who are declared by the dean of any other cathedral to be habitual worshippers at the cathedral church and whose names are not entered on the electoral roll of any parish.

Appendix III.7

7. The functions of diocesan synods

Section 4 of the Synodical Government Measure 1969 provides:

'4 (1) Diocesan synods shall be constituted for all dioceses in accordance with Part IV of the Church Representation Rules contained in Schedule 3 to this Measure and the transitional provisions contained in Schedule 4.

(2)   The functions of the diocesan synod shall be –

    (a)   to consider matters concerning the Church of England and to make provision for such matters in relation to their diocese, and to consider and express their opinion on any other matters of religious or public interest;

    (b)   to advise the bishop on any matters on which he may consult the synod;

    (c)   to consider and express their opinion on any matters referred to them by the General Synod, and in particular to approve or disapprove provisions referred to them by the General Synod under Article 8 of the Constitution:

Provided that the functions referred to in paragraph (a) hereof shall not include the issue of any statement purporting to declare the doctrine of the Church on any question.

(3)   It shall be the duty of the bishop to consult with the diocesan synod on matters of general concern and importance to the diocese.

(4)   Except as may be provided by standing orders or directions of the diocesan synod, the advisory and consultative functions of the synod under subsections (2) (b) and (3) of this section may be discharged on behalf of the synod by the bishop's council and standing committee appointed in accordance with rule 34 of the Church Representation Rules contained in Schedule 3 to this Measure, but either the bishop or the body so appointed may require any matter to be referred to the synod.

(5) The diocesan synod shall keep the deanery synods of the diocese informed of the policies and problems of the diocese and of the business which is to come before meetings of the diocesan synod, and may delegate executive functions to deanery synods; and shall keep themselves informed, through the deanery synods, of events and opinion in the parishes, and shall give opportunities of discussing at meetings of the diocesan synod matters raised by deanery synods and parochial church councils.

(6) The General Synod may by Canon or Regulation extend, amend or further define the functions of diocesan synods, and if any question arises as to whether any matter falls within the functions of a diocesan synod as laid down by subsection (2) of this section or any such Canon or Regulation relating to that subsection, it shall be decided by the bishop.

(7) As soon as a diocesan synod has been constituted, the diocesan conference shall be dissolved and all functions exercisable by the diocesan conference shall be transferred to the diocesan synod, and any reference in any Measure or instrument to diocesan conferences shall be construed as references to diocesan synods:

Provided that nothing herein shall prevent the bishop from summoning a conference of persons appearing to him to be representative of the clergy and laity of the diocese, on such occasions and for such purposes as he thinks fit.'

Appendix III.8

8. Membership of diocesan synods

Rule 30 of the Church Representation Rules provides:

'(1)   A diocesan synod shall consist of a house of bishops, a house of clergy and a house of laity.

(2)   The members of the house of bishops shall consist of the bishop of the diocese, every suffragan bishop of the diocese and such other person or persons, being a person or persons in episcopal orders working in the diocese, as the bishop of the diocese, with the concurrence of the archbishop of the province, may nominate.

(3)   The bishop of the diocese shall be the president of the diocesan synod.

(4)   The members of the house of clergy shall consist of –

    (a)   the following ex-officio members, that is to say –

        (i)   any person or persons in episcopal orders nominated by the bishop of the diocese, other than a suffragan bishop or a person nominated under paragraph (2) of this rule;

        (ii)   the dean or provost of the cathedral (including in appropriate dioceses, the Dean of Westminster, the Dean of Windsor and the Deans of Jersey and Guernsey);

        (iii)   the archdeacons;

        (iv)   the proctors elected from the diocese or from any university in the diocese (the University of London being treated for this purpose as being wholly in the diocese of London) to the Lower House of the Convocation of the Province;

        (v)   any other member of that House, being a person chosen by and from among the clerical members of religious communities in the Province, who resides in the diocese;

(vi) the chancellor of the diocese (if in Holy Orders); and

(vii) the chairman of the diocesan board of finance and the chairman of the diocesan advisory committee (if in Holy Orders);

(b) members elected by the house of clergy of the deanery synods in the diocese in accordance with the next following rules; and

(c) not more than five members (being clerks in Holy Orders) co-opted by the house of clergy of the diocesan synod.

(5) The members of the house of laity shall consist of –

(a) the following ex-officio members, that is to say –

(i) the chancellor of the diocese (if not in Holy Orders);

(ii) the chairman of the diocesan board of finance and the chairman of the diocesan advisory committee (if not in Holy Orders);

(iii) the members elected from the diocese to the House of Laity of the General Synod;

(iv) any other member of that House, being an ex-officio or co-opted member of the House of Laity of the General Synod or a person chosen by and from among the lay members of religious communities in the Province, who resides in the diocese;

(b) members elected by the houses of laity of the deanery synods in the diocese in accordance with the next following rules; and

(c) not more than five members co-opted by the house of laity of the diocesan synod, who shall be actual communicants of eighteen years or upwards.

(6) The bishop of the diocese may nominate ten additional members of the diocesan synod, who may be of the clergy or the laity and shall be members of the appropriate house. Except in regard to their appointment the nominated members shall have the same rights and be subject to the same rules as elected members. Where necessary the bishop's council and standing committee shall designate the deanery synod of which the nominated member shall be a member and, where a nominated lay person is on more than one electoral roll, he shall choose the parochial church council of which he is to be a member.

(7) No person, other than the chancellor of a diocese, shall be entitled to be a member of more than one diocesan synod at the same time.

(8) The registrar of the diocese and any deputy registrar of the diocesan synod shall be disqualified from standing to election to the diocesan synod or from being nominated, co-opted or ex-officio member of that synod.'

Appendix III.9

9. Specimen Bishop's Senior Staff Meeting Agenda

A   Consideration of names of people outside the Diocese asking for a post (about 5 per month).

B   Vacancies – there are approximately 10 vacancies on the list most months. The patronage in the Diocese is, in over 75% of parishes, in the hands of the Diocesan Bishop.

C   Collations, Institutions and Licensings – dates and allocation.

D   Curates and Layworkers – appointments, review after 1 and 3 years; the designation of parishes as ones in which deacons can be trained. (This is the implementation of a policy which was taken to, and endorsed by, the Pastoral Committee.)

E   Names & situations for consideration:

    1   Pastoral Care of Clergy: 10–15 names each month.

    2   Appointment of Army Chaplains, both TA and Cadets.

    3   Ecumenical Confirmations; guidelines.

    4   Sector Ministers and Tied Housing re Inland Revenue.

    5   Recommendation to Appointments Committee of the Bishop's Council for a Church Urban Fund Link Officer.

    6   Future use of the curate's House in Team Ministry.

    7   St Agatha's: The Old Rectory. (Present incumbent will not give notice to tenant who will not pay the rent.)

F   General Issues:

    1   Appointment of University Assistant Chaplain: Job Description.

    2   Production of a Diocesan Handbook for Clergy.

    3   Re-writing of the Inauguration of Ministry Service.

    4   Allocation of Clergy for the Diocesan Review of Ministry in which every licensed clergyperson is involved and

undertaken with one of the two bishops or two arch-deacons.

5   The Inauguration of a New LEP in a new housing area.

6   Letter to the Bishop re Millennium Fund from a Deanery Synod.

7   Appointment of a Vocations Chaplain for a Deanery.

8   Blessing of a Civil Marriage after a ceremony in a local hotel?

9   Pilgrim's Way 1997 – request from the Archbishop of Canterbury.

10   Appointment of a Chaplain to the Deaf.

11   Clergy Discipline – Code of Conduct Document.

12   Disclosure of Criminal Record process for appointments from outside the Diocese.

13   Dates for Staff Meeting in 1997.

Appendix III.10

10. Article 7 of the Constitution of the General Synod

'7 (1) A provision touching doctrinal formulae or the services or ceremonies of the Church of England or the administration of the sacraments or sacred rites thereof shall, before it is finally approved by the General Synod, be referred to the House of Bishops, and shall be submitted for such final approval in terms proposed by the House of Bishops and not otherwise.

(2) A provision touching any of the matters aforesaid shall, if the Convocations or either of them or the House of Laity so require, be referred, in the terms proposed by the House of Bishops for final approval by the General Synod, to the two Convocations sitting separately for their provinces and to the House of Laity; and no provision so referred shall be submitted for final approval by the General Synod unless it has been approved, in the terms so proposed, by each House of the two Convocations sitting as aforesaid and by the House of Laity.

(3) The question whether such a reference is required by the Convocation shall be decided by the President and Prolocutor of the Houses of that Convocation, and the Prolocutor shall consult the Standing Committee of the Lower House of Canterbury or, as the case may be, the Assessors of the Lower House of York, and the decision of the President and Prolocutor shall be conclusive;

Provided that if, before such a decision is taken, either House of Convocation resolves that the provision concerned shall be so referred or both Houses resolve that it shall not be so referred, the resolution or resolutions shall be a conclusive decision that the reference is or is not required by that Convocation.

(4) The question whether such a reference is required by the House of Laity shall be decided by the Prolocutor and Pro-Prolocutor of that House who shall consult the Standing Committee of

that House, and the decision of the Prolocutor and Pro-Prolocutor shall be conclusive;

Provided that if, before such a decision is taken, the House of Laity resolves that the reference is or is not required, the resolution shall be a conclusive decision of that question.

(5) Standing Orders of the General Synod shall provide for ensuring that a provision which fails to secure approval on a reference under this Article by each of the four Houses of the Convocations or by the House of Laity of the General Synod is not proposed again in the same or similar form until a new General Synod comes into being, except that, in the case of objection by one House of one Convocation only, provision may be made for a second reference to the Convocations and, in the case of a second objection by one House only, for reference to the Houses of Bishops and Clergy of the General Synod for approval by a two-thirds majority of the members of each House present and voting, in lieu of such approval by the four Houses aforesaid.

(6) If any question arises whether the requirements of this Article or Standing Orders made thereunder apply to any provision, or whether those requirements have been complied with, it shall be conclusively determined by the Presidents and Prolocutors of the Houses of the Convocations and the Prolocutor and Pro-Prolocutor of the House of Laity of the General Synod.'

Appendix III.11

11. Functions of the General Synod

The functions of the General Synod are set out in paragraph 6 of Schedule 2 to the Synodical Government Measure in the following terms:

'(a) To consider matters concerning the Church of England and to make provision in respect thereof –

    (i) by Measure intended to be given, in the manner prescribed by the Church of England Assembly (Powers) Act 1919, the force and effect of an Act of Parliament; or

    (ii) by Canon made, promulged and executed in accordance with the like provisions and subject to the like restrictions and having the like legislative force as Canons heretofore made, promulged and executed by the Convocations of Canterbury and York; or

    (iii) by such order, regulation or other subordinate instrument as may be authorised by Measure or Canon; or

    (iv) by such Act of Synod, regulation or other instrument or proceeding as may be appropriate in cases where provision by or under a Measure or Canon is not required.

(b) To consider and express their opinion on any other matters of religious or public interest.'

Appendix III.12

12. Canon H2 of the representation of the clergy in the Lower House of the Convocations

(This is a conflated text of two parallel Canons promulged by the Convocations of Canterbury and York. Wording which appears only in the Canterbury or the York version is distinguished by the paragraph heading or shown in square brackets.)

'Canterbury

1 Whenever the Lord Archbishop of Canterbury shall summon a Convocation of that Province, the following persons, and they only, shall henceforth be cited to appear in the Lower House of the said Convocation:

(a)   ten persons elected by and from among the Deans and Provosts of all the Cathedral Churches in the Province, the Deans of the two Collegiate Churches of St Peter in Westminster and of St George, Windsor, and the Dean of the Cathedral Church of the Holy Trinity in Gibraltar in such manner as may be provided ·by rules made under this Canon;

(b)   either the Dean of Jersey or the Dean of Guernsey as may be determined in such manner as may be provided by rules made under this Canon;

(c)   one Archdeacon in each diocese appointed in such manner as may be provided by rules made under this Canon;

(d)   the Chaplain of the Fleet, the Chaplain-General of the Forces, the Chaplain in Chief, Royal Air Force, and the Chaplain General of Prisons or, where the holder of such office is not a clerk in Holy Orders, such chaplain of the relevant Service as may be nominated by the Archbishop of Canterbury;

(e)   proctors of the clergy who shall be elected in accordance with the following provisions of this Canon;

(f)   one person chosen by and from among the clerical members of religious communities in the Province in such manner as may be provided by rules made under this Canon;

(g)   each of the following persons, if he is a clergyman, the Dean of the Arches and Auditor, the Vicar-General of the Province, the Third Church Estates Commissioner and the Chairman of the Church of England Pensions Board;

and those persons, together with any persons co-opted under paragraph 11 hereof, shall constitute the said Lower House. For the purposes of this Canon and any rules made thereunder the diocese in Europe shall be deemed to be a diocese in the Province of Canterbury and references to a diocese, except the reference in sub-paragraph (c) of this paragraph, shall be construed accordingly.

York

1   Whenever the Lord Archbishop of York shall summon a Convocation of that Province, the following persons, and they only, shall henceforth be cited to appear in the Lower House of the said Convocation:

(a)   five persons elected by and from among the Deans and Provosts of all the Cathedral Churches in the Province in such manner as may be provided by rules made under this Canon;

(b)   the Archdeacon of Man, and one Archdeacon in each diocese other than the Diocese of Sodor and Man appointed in such manner as may be provided by rules made under this Canon;

(c)   proctors of the clergy who shall be elected in accordance with the following provisions of this Canon;

(d)   one person chosen by and from among the clerical members of religious communities in the Province in such manner as may be provided by rules made under this Canon;

(e)   the Vicar-General of the Province if he is a clergyman.

and those persons, together with any person co-opted under paragraph 11 hereof, shall constitute the said Lower House.

Both Convocations

1A   A person in episcopal orders shall not be qualified to be elected, chosen or co-opted to be a member of the Lower House and no person who is a member of the House of Bishops of a diocesan synod shall be entitled to elect or choose a member or members of the Lower House; and any member of the Lower House who is ordained or consecrated as a bishop shall be deemed to have vacated his seat.

2   Each diocese in the Province shall be an electoral area, and the number of persons elected for a diocese shall be in such proportion to the number of electors in that diocese as shall be determined from time to time by the General Synod:

Provided that

(a)   the total number of proctors directly elected and specially elected from the dioceses in the Province shall not exceed [one hundred and seventy – Canterbury] [eighty – York] and no diocese shall have fewer than three directly elected proctors [except the diocese in Europe which shall have two proctors – Canterbury] [except the diocese of Sodor and Man which shall have one proctor – York]. Ex-officio and co-opted proctors shall be additional to the said total number.

In this paragraph 'proctors specially elected' means the Deans and Provosts, [the Dean of Jersey or Guernsey as the case may be, – Canterbury] the representative Archdeacons, the University proctors, and the proctors for the Religious Communities and they shall be included in the said total number;

'ex-officio proctors' means the proctors referred to in [paragraph 1 (d) and (g) – Canterbury] [paragraph 1 (e) – York] of this Canon; and

'co-opted proctors' means the proctors referred to in paragraph 11 of this Canon.

(b)   it shall be competent for the Archbishop of the province on the petition of the electors in any diocese to divide the diocese into electoral areas and to assign a number of proctors to each area from the number allowed to the whole diocese; the division and assignment to be made in such manner that no electoral area will have fewer than three proctors and the number of proctors assigned to each area will be proportionate to the number of electors within that area.

Canterbury

3   The Universities in the Province shall constitute four electoral areas:

(a)   the University of Oxford,

(b)   the University of Cambridge,

(c)   the University of London,

(d)   the other Universities in the Province acting together for this purpose;

and one proctor shall be elected for each such electoral area.

York

3   The Universities in the Province shall constitute two electoral areas:

(a)   the Universities of Durham and Newcastle acting together for this purpose;

(b)   the other Universities in the Province acting together for this purpose;

and one proctor shall be elected for each such electoral area.

Both Convocations

4   The electors shall be:

(a)   where a diocese or part thereof is the electoral area, all clergymen exercising the office of Assistant Bishop in the area, or beneficed in the area, or holding office in a Cathedral Church [or in one of the aforesaid Collegiate Churches situated – Canterbury] in the area, or licensed under seal by the Bishop of the diocese, not being a member of the House of Bishops of the diocesan synod, Deans or Provosts, Archdeacons, [the Chaplains mentioned in para. 1 (d) hereof – Canterbury], the electors mentioned in the next sub-paragraph, or members of the religious communities;

(b) where a University or group of Universities is the electoral area, all clergymen having the qualifications specified in rules made under this Canon.'

Appendix III.13

13. House of Laity of General Synod

Membership of the House of Laity of the General Synod is prescribed by the Church Representation Rules as follows:

'Membership of House of Laity

35 (1) The House of Laity of the General Synod shall consist of –

    (a) the members elected by the diocesan electors of each diocese as hereinafter provided;

    (b) three members, two from the Province of Canterbury and one from the Province of York, chosen by the lay members of religious communities from among their number in such manner as may be provided by a resolution of the General Synod;

    (c) such ex-officio and co-opted members as are hereinafter provided.

(2) For the purposes of this Part of these rules the diocese in Europe shall be deemed to be a diocese in the Province of Canterbury.

(3) For the purposes of this Part of these rules, the diocesan electors of a diocese other than the diocese in Europe shall be the members of the houses of laity of all the deanery synods in the diocese other than –

    (a) persons co-opted to the deanery synod under rule 24 (7); or

    (b) persons who are lay members of a religious community with separate representation in the General Synod under paragraph 1 (b) of this rule.

(4) The diocesan electors of the diocese in Europe shall be such number of persons elected by the annual meetings of the chaplaincies in the said diocese as may be determined by the bishop's council and standing committee of the said diocese, and any lay person who is –

(a)   an actual communicant as defined in rule 54 (1);

(b)   of eighteen years or upwards; and

(c)   a person whose name is entered on the electoral roll of such a chaplaincy;

shall be qualified for election as a diocesan elector by the annual meeting of that chaplaincy.

(5)   The qualifying date for lay members of religious communities under paragraph (1) (b) of this rule and for diocesan electors under paragraphs (3) and (4) of this rule shall be 6.00 am on the date of the dissolution of the General Synod, save that when a casual vacancy is being filled, the qualifying date shall be 6.00 am on the date on which the nomination papers are issued.

(6)   The register of lay electors shall be open to inspection at the diocesan office and any errors and omissions in the list may be corrected until the close of nominations. Thereafter no names may be added or removed until the declaration of the result of the election and those persons whose names are entered in the register shall be the qualified electors entitled to vote in that election.'

'42   (1)   The following persons, if they are not in Holy Orders, shall be ex-officio members of the House of Laity –

(a)   the Dean of the Arches and Auditor;

(b)   the Vicar-General of the Province of Canterbury;

(c)   the Vicar-General of the Province of York;

(d)   the three Church Estates Commissioners;

(e)   the Chairman of the Central Board of Finance;

(f)   the Chairman of the Church of England Pensions Board.

2   The House of Laity shall have power to co-opt persons who are actual lay communicants of eighteen years or upwards to be members of the House of Laity:

Provided that –

(a) the co-opted members shall not at any time exceed five in number; and

(b) no person shall be qualified to become a co-opted member unless not less than two-thirds of the members of the Standing Committee of the House of Laity shall have first consented to his being co-opted, either at a meeting of the Standing Committee or in writing.

(3) Except in regard to their appointment, the ex-officio and co-opted members shall have the same rights and be subject to the same rules and regulations as elected members. Where such members are on more than one electoral roll, they shall choose the parochial church council of which they are to be a member.

(4) Co-opted members shall continue to be members of the House of Laity until the next dissolution of the General Synod, but without prejudice to their acting under Article 3 (4) of the Constitution during the period of the dissolution or to their continuing to be ex-offico members of other bodies constituted under these rules during that period:

Provided that the House of Laity may, in the case of any co-opted member, fix a shorter period of membership.

(5) The House of Laity may make standing orders for regulating the procedure of and incidental to the appointment of co-opted members, and otherwise for carrying this rule into effect.'

Appendix III.14

14. Composition of the General Synod in 1995

	Canterbury	York	Either Province	TOTAL
House of Bishops				
Diocesan Bishops	30	14		44
Suffragan Bishops	6	3		9
	36	17		53
House of Clergy				
Deans or Provosts	10	5		15
Archdeacons	29	14		43
Service Chaplains and Chaplain General of Prisons	4			4
Elected Proctors and the Dean of Guernsey or Jersey	126	58		184
University Proctors	4	2		6
Religious	1	1		2
Co-opted places	3	2		5
	177	82		259
House of Laity				
Elected Laity	168	79		247
Religious	2	1		3
Co-opted places			5	5
Ex-officio (First and Second Church Estates Commissioners and Chairman CBF)			3	3
	170	80	8	258
Either House of Clergy or House of Laity				
Ex-officio (Dean of the Arches, the 2 Vicars General, the Third Church Estates Commissioner and the Chairman of the Pensions Board)			5	5
TOTAL	383	179	13	575

Seven representatives of other Churches have been appointed to the Synod under its Standing Orders with speaking but not voting rights.

Appendix III.15

15. Election of proctors for universities

The Clergy Representation Rules provide as follows:

'12   The electors shall be priests or deacons of the Church of England who are qualified as follows –

(a)   in the University of Oxford are members of the Congregations;

(b)   in the University of Cambridge are members of the Regent House;

(c)   in the University of London are –

(i)   certified by the academic registrar to be appointed or recognised teachers of the university holding full-time posts or part-time posts declared by the holders to be their main employment;

(ii)   certified by the principal of the university or the head of the school concerned to be members of the financial and administrative staffs employed full-time by the university or by one of its schools;

(d)   in the other universities comprised in an electoral area are certified by the vice-chancellor or the university official designated by him for the purposes to be –

(i)   appointed or recognised teachers of the university holding full-time posts declared by the holders to be their main employment;

(ii)   members of the financial and administrative staffs employed full-time by the university;

and who held the qualifying membership post or employment at 6.00 am on the date of the dissolution of Convocation.'

Appendix III.16

16. Directly elected membership of Houses of Clergy and Laity of the General Synod (excluding all 'special constituencies')

Dioceses	House of Clergy		House of Laity	
	Elected in 1995	As proposed in para. 8.60	Elected in 1995	As proposed in para. 8.60
Canterbury	3	3	3	3
London	10	7	8	5
Winchester	4	3	9	4
Bath and Wells	4	3	8	5
Birmingham	3	3	3	3
Bristol	3	3	4	3
Chelmsford	6	5	9	6
Chichester	6	4	11	7
Coventry	3	3	3	3
Derby	3	3	4	3
Ely	3	3	4	3
Europe	2	2	2	2
Exeter	5	3	6	4
Gloucester	3	3	5	3
Guildford	4	3	5	3
Hereford	3	3	3	3
Leicester	3	3	3	3
Lichfield	6	4	9	6
Lincoln	4	3	5	3
Norwich	3	3	5	3
Oxford	8	6	10	6
Peterborough	3	3	4	3
Portsmouth	3	3	3	3
Rochester	4	3	6	3
St Albans	6	4	9	5
St Edmundsbury and Ipswich	3	3	4	3
Salisbury	4	3	8	5
Southwark	7	6	8	5
Truro	3	3	3	3
Worcester	3	3	4	3
Allocation to Canterbury Province	125	104	168	114

Dioceses	House of Clergy		House of Laity	
	Elected in 1995	As proposed in para. 8.60	Elected in 1995	As proposed in para. 8.60
York	6	3	8	4
Durham	5	3	6	3
Blackburn	5	3	9	5
Bradford	3	3	3	3
Carlisle	3	3	5	3
Chester	6	3	10	6
Liverpool	5	3	7	4
Manchester	6	4	8	4
Newcastle	3	3	4	3
Ripon	3	3	5	3
Sheffield	4	3	4	3
Sodor and Man	1	1	1	1
Southwell	4	3	4	3
Wakefield	4	3	5	3
Allocation to York Province	58	41	79	48
GRAND TOTAL	183	145	247	162

Appendix IV

Methods of election

1   Two methods of election are permitted in the Church of England; the simple majority, popularly known as 'first-past-the-post', and a method of proportional representation, namely the single transferable vote (STV). In elections to the Convocations and to the House of Laity of the General Synod, elections by STV are mandatory.[1]

2   The STV method of election had been adopted for elections to the House of Laity of the Church Assembly in 1920 and was probably used by the Convocations before that. No records survive to indicate why this was the preferred method in those early years.

3   The Hodson Commission, whose report *Synodical Government in the Church of England* was published in 1966, referred to the Church's voting system in the following terms:

> 'Both clerical and lay elections are conducted in accordance with the principle of proportional representation by the method of the single transferable vote. This system is often criticised on the grounds that it is extremely complicated and seldom fully comprehended by electors, candidates or even presiding officers. There is a good deal of substance in this objection. On the other hand there is no doubt that it is the only system which gives due weight to the votes of minorities and that it does ensure that where more than one person has to be elected for a constituency, the total representation more accurately reflects the various shades of opinion than might be the case were the system to be one of straight voting. We would not therefore wish to recommend any change.'[2]

---

1 See Convocations (Election to Upper House) Rules 1989 to 1994, rule 4; Clergy Representation Rules 1975 to 1994, rule 20 (6); Church Representation Rules, rule 39 (8).

2 Hodson, *Synodical Government in the Church of England,* p. 24 Central Board of Finance, 1966.

4   Some of the criticisms outlined in the Hodson Report remain valid. It is still the case that most people are used to putting a cross rather than numbers on a ballot paper, and the counting of votes in an STV election can be complicated. However, on this latter point, the Electoral Reform Society produced in 1993 a computer program which makes the counting process easier. Once all the voters' preferences have been entered into the computer, the presiding officer simply has to press a button to have an election result in seconds.

5   In the 1995 elections to the General Synod over half the dioceses took advantage of the computer program. It is anticipated that, by the election in 2000, most if not all dioceses will be using this method.

6   Another reason for using the program is that when a casual vacancy occurs in the two years following an election with voting papers, the rules require the vacancy to be filled by re-counting those voting papers. It is far easier and quicker to conduct the by-election where STV papers have been entered into the computer. The names of the former candidates who indicate that they wish to stand in the by-election are entered and the result is speedily produced by the computer. In a first-past-the-post re-count, the voting papers would have to be re-allocated to the continuing candidates and counted *de novo*.

7   It may help to outline the rudiments of the STV system. In essence each voter has one vote but he or she expresses this by denoting subsequent choices should the candidate of his or her first choice not be elected. If the first choice is excluded for lack of support the whole vote will be transferred to the second choice adding to that person's total. This continues until a candidate is elected so that, in a real sense, every voter should have a successful candidate of his choice. Where a candidate is elected (i.e. he or she achieves the quota[3]) but has a surplus of votes, only that proportion of each person's vote which was necessary to elect the candidate will be used, leaving the unused proportion of the vote to be transferred to the next choice of each voter.

---

3   The quota is the number of votes required to guarantee the election of a candidate.

8   The counting of votes in a first-past-the-post election can be a quicker process than the count in an STV election if, in the view of Canon Michael Hodge, 'no recount is necessary. If the votes have to be recounted in a simple majority election there is no alternative but to start again at the beginning. Under STV the system of checking and counter-checking at each stage ensures that, at the most, it is only necessary to re-count at the particular stage.'[4]

9   As can be seen from the quotation from the Hodson Report in paragraph 3 above, it has always been a primary argument in favour of the use of the STV method in synodical elections that it protects the interests of minorities. Since the Church has three main streams of churchmanship and given that elections are conducted on the basis of multi-member constituencies (viz. the dioceses), the STV method does give due weight to minority groups. There are still different points of view within the Church which need to be represented in the General Synod and, as we perceive it, such representation cannot be guaranteed in a first-past-the-post election.

10   The Elections Review Group of the General Synod (the body charged with monitoring elections and making recommendations for amendments to the Church Representation Rules) has stated that, in an STV election, the ideal number of places to be filled should not be fewer than three.

---

4   Hodge, M. R., *Choose! Or* (1995) p. 3.

Appendix V

The Ecclesiastical Committee

A paper prepared by Lord Bridge of Harwich

1   By the Church of England Assembly (Powers) Act 1919 (the 1919 Act), Parliament conferred on the Assembly, as the Church's representative body, the power to legislate by Measure. When the Church Assembly was succeeded by the General Synod in pursuance of the Synodical Government Measure 1969 the legislative power passed to the Synod, but the 1919 Act was not amended save that references in the 1919 Act to the Church Assembly and its Legislative Committee were to be construed as references to the General Synod and its Legislative Committee. Hence the procedure to be applied to a Measure which has been passed by the General Synod before it obtains the approval of Parliament is that laid down by the 1919 Act. Dominating this procedure are the functions conferred on the Ecclesiastical Committee, a body established by the 1919 Act consisting of fifteen members of the House of Lords appointed by the Lord Chancellor and fifteen members of the House of Commons appointed by the Speaker. The purpose of this study is to consider the legislative origins and the present-day practical operation of the Ecclesiastical Committee.

2   Briefly, the statutory procedure is as follows. A Measure passed by the Synod is first submitted by the Legislative Committee of the Synod to the Ecclesiastical Committee 'with such comments and explanations as the Legislative Committee may deem expedient or be directed by the General Synod to add:' section 3 (1). The Ecclesiastical Committee will normally hear the evidence of one or more witnesses from the Synod with reference to the policy considerations underlying the Measure in amplification of the comments and explanations of the Legislative Committee. The Ecclesiastical

Committee, either of its own motion or at the request of the Legislative Committee, may invite the Legislative Committee to a conference to discuss the Measure: section 3 (2). Such a conference has only rarely been held; it is normally considered unnecessary unless some members of the Ecclesiastical Committee hold strong views in opposition to the Measure. Having considered the Measure, the Ecclesiastical Committee is to draft a report thereon to Parliament 'stating the nature and legal effect of the measure and its views as to the expediency thereof, especially with relation to the constitutional rights of all His Majesty's subjects:' section 3 (3). The Ecclesiastical Committee's report is first submitted in draft to the Legislative Committee of the Synod and it rests with the Legislative Committee to determine whether to withdraw the Measure or to lay the Ecclesiastical Committee's report together with the text of the Measure before Parliament. The Measure and the report are then considered by each House of Parliament and upon an affirmative resolution of each House to that effect the Measure is presented to Her Majesty and upon receiving the Royal Assent has the same force and effect as an Act of Parliament: section 4.

3   The Bill which became the 1919 Act was first introduced in the House of Lords. In its passage through both Houses the Bill was substantially amended and the procedural machinery now on the statute book is significantly different from that proposed in the Bill as first presented. In the original text the Ecclesiastical Committee was to consist of 'such members of the Privy Council, not exceeding twenty-five in all, as His Majesty from time to time may think fit to appoint in that behalf.' After considering a Measure submitted to it by the Legislative Committee of the Church Assembly, and possibly discussing it in conference with the Committee, the Ecclesiastical Committee was required to 'draft a report thereon to His Majesty, advising that the Royal Assent ought or ought not to be given to it, and stating the reasons for such advice.' It was for the Legislative Committee to determine whether and when to submit the Ecclesiastical Committee's report to His Majesty, but once they had done so they were then to lay both the report and the text of the Measure before

Parliament. The Measure would then receive the Royal Assent if the Ecclesiastical Committee had so advised, unless within a given time limit either House of Parliament directed to the contrary. If the Ecclesiastical Committee had advised against the Measure, it would only receive the Royal Assent if both Houses of Parliament so directed. It will be seen that under this scheme originally proposed in the Bill the Ecclesiastical Committee was not only differently constituted, but would have played a much more important role than the Ecclesiastical Committee under the Act as passed. Its report would have been not merely advisory but determinative of the fate of a Measure in the absence of positive parliamentary action.

4   At the Committee stage of the Bill in the House of Lords the primary controversy was a constitutional one. Viscount Haldane objected to a Committee of the Privy Council advising the Sovereign, a role which he contended only a minister of the Crown responsible to Parliament should take. In an attempt, in some degree, to meet this objection an amendment was moved by Viscount Finlay to remove the provision for the Ecclesiastical Committee's report to advise the Sovereign whether or not the Royal Assent ought to be given to a Measure and substituting the language now found in the Act of 1919 requiring that the Ecclesiastical Committee's report state 'its views as to the expediency [of the Measure], especially with relation to the constitutional rights of all His Majesty's subjects.' Giving advice in this case, it was contended by Viscount Finlay and others, was an entirely appropriate function for a Committee of the Privy Council to perform. This amendment having been agreed to, the provision for the fate of a Measure to follow automatically on the Ecclesiastical Committee's advice in the absence of parliamentary intervention had also to be amended and it was now provided instead that a Measure should only receive the Royal Assent if both Houses of Parliament affirmatively so resolved.

5   It was clearly appreciated in the course of the debates on the Bill in both Houses of Parliament that the legislative power sought by the Church Assembly could not be confined to matters which exclusively concerned the Church of England, but must not infrequently

overlap with areas of secular concern. Indeed, when the Bill was before the Standing Committee of the House of Commons, an amendment which would have confined the subject matter to which Measures might relate to 'any matter exclusively concerning the Church of England' was withdrawn after full argument in debate. The promoters of the Bill were well aware that, in so far as Church of England legislation might have an impact on interests outside those of the Church, it was important that such interests should be adequately safeguarded. The debate at the Committee stage of the Bill in the House of Lords shows what importance was attached to the proposed role of the Ecclesiastical Committee in this regard and why it was thought that a Committee of the Privy Council could most effectively discharge that role. The Marquess of Salisbury said:

'The procedure which the promoters propose is this – that as soon as the Church Assembly, through its committee, has arrived at its conclusions, and before the matter is submitted to Parliament, the suggested Bill should go to a very important and absolutely impartial Committee of experts, who should look into the proposal and see whether, in point of fact, it is open to any objection from the point of view of the general rights of His Majesty's subjects or from that of any technical consideration of which they may be masters. For that purpose you want an expert Committee, and a Committee which deserves and obtains the full confidence of public opinion and of Parliament. The promoters have looked where I think they ought to have looked – to the members of His Majesty's Privy Council – to furnish such a body. It is not suggested that they should be advocates of the Church in any sense – the Committee may contain the noble and learned Lord himself – but the members should know the whole history of Constitutional law and the history of the law which concerns the relations between the Church and the State, as well as the various matters which it is important to safeguard in the interests of His Majesty's

177

subjects at large. The Privy Council contains such men. It contains all the men who are the greatest in that respect which the Kingdom can produce. Therefore, the promoters thought that out of that body could be created a Committee which should do this very work.' (House of Lords Reports, 10 July 1919, columns 434–5)

The Earl of Selborne said:

'With the utmost good-will and honest intention in the world it is surely highly probable that in dealing with the Ecclesiastical laws of the country as they exist at present the Church Assembly may fail to notice the full effect of some change which they may wish to propose to Parliament. We felt that, if we wished the measures proposed by the Church Assembly to acquire a good reputation with Parliament for their moderation and their strict respect for the constitutional rights of all His Majesty's subjects, we should wish to have these proposals pass the test of a body whose judgement could not be impugned or whose adequacy for the task could not be questioned, and we invented, if I may use that term, this Ecclesiastical Committee of the Privy Council, so that when a measure comes it may come accompanied by a Report telling the Cabinet, Parliament, the Public and the Press the full legal and ultimate effect of every measure proposed by the Church Assembly, and especially what the effect is going to be on the rights of His Majesty's subjects as citizens of the Realm.' (House of Lords Reports, 10 July 1919, columns 440–1)

6   When the Bill came before a Standing Committee in the House of Commons the constitution of the Ecclesiastical Committee from members of the Privy Council again came under challenge, but this time from a very different point of view from that which had prompted Viscount Haldane's objection. An amendment was now proposed that the Ecclesiastical Committee should be a joint Committee of both Houses of Parliament. The motive seems to have

been political and primary support for the proposal appears to have come from those who spoke in the interests of non-conformist Christian denominations. Sir Ryland Adkins, moving the basic amendment, said:

> 'What we want is, that there shall be a Joint Committee, chosen with the utmost care, really representative in character, on which large sections of the community who may not be in full or constant communion with the Established Church may feel that their point of view is adequately represented, and, what is infinitely more important than the desires of any section of the country, that the wisdom of Parliament representing the whole community may be brought to bear in a convenient, practical, and influential way upon Bills, presented under the terms of this Bill, at the earliest moment and in a way which would facilitate and not hinder prompt progress when it had been so investigated.' (House of Commons – Standing Committee Reports, 19 November 1919, columns 636–7)

The promoters of the Bill evidently had considerable misgivings as to the suitability of a Joint Parliamentary Committee to perform the role envisaged for the Ecclesiastical Committee and initially opposed the amendment. Viscount Wolmer said of the Committee:

> 'It must not be tainted with any suspicion of partiality or partisanship. It must be an impartial body, and it must also be a body that is strong in legal learning, so that the legal effect of the Bill can be clearly set forth, and set forth with authority. . . . What I am afraid about in my hon. Friend's proposal – I do not say that this difficulty is insurmountable – is that the atmosphere of partisanship should creep into these Joint Parliamentary Committees. That is a thing which should be avoided at all costs. . . . Therefore it is very important to provide against the Committee which is to advise Parliament being composed of men with a partisan axe to grind,

179

either for the Church or against the Government. The Committee must be impartial and must be judicial.' (House of Commons – Standing Committee Reports, 19 November 1919, from columns 641 & 642)

Lord Hugh Cecil said of the Committee:

'We want it to be the best safeguard for the proper rights and control of the State, by giving Parliament all the light on the subject that can be given. We want it certainly, if there is any danger in that direction, to guard the rights of all persons who do not conform to the worship and discipline of the Church of England. We want it, finally, to give its skilled assistance in making sure that measures propounded by the National Assembly of the Church of England really do effect through the intricate machinery of ecclesiastical law, the purposes which that Assembly has in view.' (House of Commons – Standing Committee Reports, 19 November 1919, column 643)

But after lengthy debate, evidently in the interests of avoiding any semblance of political conflict, the promoters gave way on this issue and so it came about that the constitution of the Ecclesiastical Committee came to be that which is now embodied in the Act of 1919. Reading the debates in both Houses of Parliament on the passage of the Bill which became the Act of 1919, it is clear that, however the Ecclesiastical Committee was to be constituted, no one on either side ever contemplated that the role of the Ecclesiastical Committee in expressing 'its view as to the expediency' of a Measure would be to express a view contradicting or over-riding the view reached by the Church Assembly, as the Church's own representative body, on a pure issue of Church policy.

7   Since the Synodical Government Measure 1969 came into operation there has been no occasion when the Ecclesiastical Committee has communicated a draft report on a Measure to the Legislative Committee of the Synod pursuant to section 3 (3) and (4) of the 1919 Act which expressed the view that the Measure was

inexpedient. There have, however, been a number of occasions when the Chairman of the Ecclesiastical Committee or Counsel to the Chairman of the Committee in the House of Lords, as the Ecclesiastical Committee's legal adviser, has informally communicated to the General Synod's advisers some technical objection to the drafting of a Measure which has resulted in the Measure being withdrawn and later re-submitted in a revised form. Only one Measure submitted for parliamentary approval has failed in due course to gain the necessary approval of both Houses. This was the Appointment of Bishops Measure. The Measure was laid before Parliament on 18 June 1984 together with the Ecclesiastical Committee's report, which expressed the view without reservation that the Measure was expedient. A resolution that the Measure be presented for the Royal Assent was nevertheless defeated in the House of Commons by 32 votes to 17 in a vote taken at 12.21 am on 17 July 1984. This Measure was never debated in the House of Lords.

8   Traditionally the Chairman of the Ecclesiastical Committee has always been a present or retired Lord of Appeal in Ordinary and there has only been one contested election to the Chair. This was at the commencement in 1992 of the last Parliament when Lord Templeman was in the event elected. The Second Church Estates Commissioner, who speaks for the Church Commissioners in the House of Commons and who normally moves any resolution in the House of Commons that a Measure submitted by the General Synod be presented to Her Majesty for the Royal Assent, is also always a member of the Ecclesiastical Committee. It is probably true to say that the remaining membership of the Committee in recent times has been determined rather by the ascertainment of those willing to serve than by any careful process of selection carried out by the Lord Chancellor and the Speaker. This has quite naturally resulted in most of the members of the Committee being active members of the Church of England with a keen interest in its affairs, and over the years a number of members of the Ecclesiastical Committee have also been members of the General Synod. Again quite naturally, the opinions of members of the Committee tend approximately to correspond to a cross-section of opinion in the Church of England at large, and

are often strongly held.

9   It is instructive to take note of the proceedings in the Ecclesiastical Committee in relation to the two most controversial Measures of recent times, namely the Clergy (Ordination) Measure 1990 and the Priests (Ordination of Women) Measure 1993, and to note the circumstances in which those Measures eventually secured parliamentary approval.

10   Prior to the Clergy (Ordination) Measure it was an absolute bar to a man's ordination to the priesthood that, being married to a second wife, his former spouse was still living or that his wife had a former spouse still living. The sole purpose of the Measure was to enable an Archbishop, on the application of a diocesan bishop, in an exceptional case to grant a dispensation from this absolute disqualification. The long history leading up to the Measure need not be recited here. At the end of the day there remained an acute difference of view in the Church as to its propriety. But the Measure was passed by the General Synod, acting entirely in accordance with its constitution, by votes of 29 to 5 in the House of Bishops, 139 to 65 in the House of Clergy and 125 to 77 in the House of Laity. The Measure was considered by the Ecclesiastical Committee at six meetings between March 1988 and April 1989. At one of these meetings evidence was received from representatives of Synod; at another the Ecclesiastical Committee met in conference with the Legislative Committee of the Synod. At the last meeting of the Ecclesiastical Committee, when the terms of the statutory report pursuant to section 3 (3) of the 1919 Act were finally settled, of the members present and voting 10 were of the view that the Measure was expedient, 9 that it was inexpedient. In substance the difference of view in the Ecclesiastical Committee reflected the difference of view in the Synod, in the sense that the issue on which they were divided was precisely the same, and the debates in the Ecclesiastical Committee were, in large measure, a repetition of debates in the Synod. When the Archbishop of Canterbury moved in the House of Lords that the Measure be submitted to Her Majesty for the Royal Assent, an amendment, in effect to reject the Measure, was the subject of a lively

debate but was not pressed to a division, and the Archbishop's motion was agreed to without a division. But when it was first moved in the House of Commons that the Measure be presented for the Royal Assent, the Measure was the subject of a debate commencing at 2.06 am on 18 July 1989 and when the vote was taken at 3.26 am the Measure was rejected by 51 votes to 45. However, in the next Session of Parliament the Measure was again the subject of a motion that it be presented for the Royal Assent and this time the debate commenced at 10.15 pm on 20 February 1990. When the vote was taken at 11.45 pm there was, not surprisingly, a larger attendance than there had been on the occasion of the debate in July 1989 and this time the motion was carried by 228 votes to 106.

11   The controversial issue surrounding the Priests (Ordination of Women) Measure 1993 is well within the recollection of us all. In accordance with Article 8 of the Constitution of the General Synod, the Measure was submitted to and approved by 38 out of 44 diocesan synods. The final voting in the General Synod in favour of the Measure was by 39 to 13 in the House of Bishops, 176 to 74 in the House of Clergy and 169 to 82 in the House of Laity, thus providing the majority of two-thirds of those present and voting in each House required for the final approval of the Measure under Article 8. The Ecclesiastical Committee considered the Measure together with the Ordination of Women (Financial Provisions) Measure 1993, at eleven meetings between 22 March and 19 July 1993. At four of these meetings, extending over a total period of ten hours, the Committee received evidence from representatives of the General Synod. One meeting was held in conference with the Legislative Committee of the General Synod. In the final voting on the Priests (Ordination of Women) Measure 16 members were of the view that the Measure was expedient, 11 that it was inexpedient. A substantial part of the Ecclesiastical Committee's time was no doubt devoted to the provisions of the main Measure designed to safeguard the position of those in the Church of England who were conscientiously unable to accept the ministration of women priests and to the provisions for compensation in the Financial Provisions Measure. But here again it is clear that the central issue concerning and dividing the members of the

Ecclesiastical Committee and the issue to which much of the debate was devoted was precisely the same issue which had divided the General Synod, namely the propriety of allowing women to be ordained to the priesthood in the Church of England at all. In the House of Lords an amendment to the motion that the Priests (Ordination of Women) Measure be presented to Her Majesty for the Royal Assent, which would have had the effect at least of postponing its enactment, was defeated by 135 votes to 25. The motions that both the Priests (Ordination of Women) Measure and the Ordination of Women (Financial Provisions) Measure be presented to Her Majesty for the Royal Assent were both agreed to without division. In the House of Commons the corresponding motions relating to the two Measures were affirmed by 215 to 21 and 195 to 19 votes respectively.

12   It is apparent that the present constitution of the Ecclesiastical Committee and the functions prescribed for it by the 1919 Act tend to promote lengthy and vigorous debate in the Committee of the most controversial issues of Church policy which have divided the Synod and eventually been resolved there. It is a question which may merit consideration whether this intermediate level of debate between the General Synod on the one hand and the two Houses of Parliament on the other hand makes a necessary or useful contribution to the legislative process. There seems no reason to doubt, however, that the examination to which Measures are subjected by the Ecclesiastical Committee adequately provides the safeguards which were envisaged as necessary by the promoters of the 1919 legislation, albeit that those safeguards might be provided more expeditiously and economically by a body with a different constitution and different statutory terms of reference.